THE COMPLETE GUIDE TO GETTING A TEACHING JOB

ADAM WAXLER
and
MARJAN GLAVAC

Previously published as an eBook:

Your Basic Guide to Acing ANY Teacher Interview

© 2019 Marjan Glavac

Title: The Complete Guide to Getting A Teaching Job

Format: Paperback

This publication has been assigned: 978-1-9991631-1-2

Title: The Complete Guide to Getting A Teaching Job

Format: Electronic book

This publication has been assigned: 978-1-9991631-2-9

Interior Design and Formatting: Ruslan Nabiev

For free resources for getting a teaching job, becoming an effective teacher and making teaching fun, visit:

www.TheBusyEducator.com

Table of Contents

About the Author Adam Waxler

Hello Busy Educator,

I wanted to start by introducing myself and letting you know why I feel I am qualified to help you land that perfect teaching job!

My name is Adam Waxler. I retired from full-time teaching as a middle school social studies teacher, adjunct education professor, and teacher mentor. I am also the author of several teaching books and websites.

While living in New York I spent six years at Springs School, a small K-8 district on the East End of Long Island in the town of East Hampton. While teaching at Springs, I was not only involved with our new teacher-training program, but also played an active role in teacher recruitment.

For many reasons, I was in a unique situation. During my years at Springs School, there happened to be quite a bit of hiring taking place. One reason for this was the large turnover rate the school unfortunately faced. The reason for the large turnover was not necessarily the fault of the school, but rather a fault with the system as a whole. On the East End of Long Island the school districts are faced with something known as "district hopping".

So what is district hopping?

First, I must explain that the school districts in New York are relatively small compared to many other states in the country. Unlike many other states in which the entire county makes up one school district, in New York one small town can have several school districts within it.

For example, the small town of East Hampton, with a year-round population of 18,000, has four different school districts, each with their own superintendent, principal, and school board.

What does this have to do with teacher recruitment and "district hopping"?

Everything!

Each of these districts has its own unique contract. Where you start on that contract (*which step you start on*) is completely negotiable! Therefore, if you are working at one district as a Spanish teacher and a Spanish teacher from another school district five minutes down the road retires, you may very well "hop" to the open position for more money. But this isn't a given. It depends on applying, going through the interview process and being offered the job. Being qualified is an excellent first step. The other district must post this job to teachers outside their own district in order for you to apply. Finally, you have to be deemed the best choice by members of the hiring committee. The committee considers education, experience and your ability to convince them that you understand the job and are their best choice.

This "district hopping" is such common practice that many schools (especially those who can't compete with the higher paying districts) are constantly recruiting new teachers. And, as you may have guessed, Springs School was one of those school districts which often lost good teachers to better paying school districts.

At the same time, the Springs School community was rapidly growing. Therefore, during my tenure at Springs School, we were adding new teachers in each subject area and at every grade level.

The combination of "district hopping" and rapid expansion put me in a unique position. I played an active role in teacher recruitment by sitting on several interview committees each year for various subject areas and various grade levels. Not only did I participate in the initial screening of resumes and cover letters, but I also would sit in on the initial interview. I observed demonstration lessons, and any follow up on interviews before giving my final recommendation to the principal and superintendent.

While *I* obviously knew what *I* was looking for when conducting an interview with a potential new staff member, by participating in these interview committees, I became well aware of what *other* teachers were looking for as well. Believe me, it was not always the same thing. In fact, I have heard some of the strangest interview questions you can imagine. I also became well aware of the most common interview questions AND the best way to answer those questions.

Interestingly, I recently found myself on the other side of the table as my wife and I decided to move from the dreary New York winters. *(Sorry, New Yorkers! But you know it's true!)* We set our sights on the sunny beaches of Florida. I resigned from a great position at Springs School and entered the job hunt with thousands of other teachers. I discovered that, while I had often heard there was a need for teachers in Florida, the fact was that there were literally no social studies positions available in any of the areas where we wanted to live. In fact, at the Lee County job fair in 2005, attended by over 3,000 teachers, the county was not offering a single social studies contract at that time. When I finally did get an interview at Haile Middle School in Bradenton, Florida (my former place of employment) I was told in no uncertain terms that I was one of 140 applicants for that one social studies position.

So, how did I get the job? How did I even get offered an interview in the first place?

That's exactly what I am going to share with you in this eBook. I decided to put everything I know about interviews, gained from both sides of the table, into this one publication. In doing so I hope to help other teachers land that perfect teaching job ... the teaching job of their dreams.

While I may be able to give you inside tips and tricks on how to ace your interview, nothing substitutes for having a working knowledge of the most effective teaching strategies, an excellent teaching track record, and stellar references from employers past and present.

In addition to my involvement with teacher recruitment, I also played a big role in new teacher training. I currently own and operate several teaching websites that provide simple teaching strategies and teaching tips to help improve classroom management, increase class participation, and improve academic achievement (including performance on standardized tests).

Good luck with your job search!

About the Author Marjan Glavac

My name is Marjan Glavac and I'd like to help you find your dream teaching job.

I'm the author of 4 teacher books, co-author of a complete teacher training system and the co-author of the very successful book The Complete Guide to Getting A Teaching Job.

I was also a classroom teacher for 29 years.

I've made every mistake in the book when it came to looking for a job.

When I graduated with my B.A., I sent out 100 personalized cover letters with customized resumes.

One hundred letters and resumes! I received zero offers. I was devastated.

Two years later, I sent out a handful of letters and ultimately beat out thousands of candidates to land my dream teaching job.

I learned a lot in those two years—and more in the years since—and I'd like to share it with you.

I've been on hiring committees. I've read hundreds of resumes and cover letters.

I've picked the mind of administrators to find out what they were looking for in a teacher.

And this is something I've always had a passion for.

Before I got into teaching, I had a minor in Personnel and Industrial Relations at the university level.

Teaching for 29 years for 2 school districts and 7 schools gave me a lot of experience at interviewing and landing teacher jobs that I wanted.

I paid attention, and now I've got a career's worth of experience to share with you.

My YouTube channel, newsletters, and websites have helped thousands of teachers like yourself find a teaching job.

Together with my co-author Adam Waxler, we've been on countless hiring committees. We've read hundreds of resumes and cover letters. We have been responsible for hiring (or not hiring) new staff members in various content areas at different grade levels.

We learned from administrators what they were really looking for in a teacher.

The same tips and strategies that we both used to get our dream teaching jobs are contained in this book.

We're here to help you land your dream teaching job.

Introduction

Teaching is a wonderful profession whose rewards go beyond a simple paycheck ... way beyond. However, in order to experience this, you first have to get the job.

Whether you are an aspiring student teacher looking for that first job or a seasoned veteran looking to relocate, interviewing for a teaching position can be an extremely daunting task to say the least.

Everything that you could ever want may be riding on your behavior at that interview and the smallest thing can mean the difference between having a new teaching position, or being back to "pounding the pavement".

As someone who sat on several interview committees each year, I am often amazed at how it can be the smallest detail that causes people to fail the interview.

Fortunately, there are many things you can and should be doing to ease the pressure and to help secure that teaching position you desire.

This book is your comprehensive guide to winning the teaching job of your dreams. In it you will learn:

- Where to search for teaching jobs.
- How to get the interview of your choice.
- How to prepare for the interview.
- How to make a great first impression.

- How to conduct yourself during the interview.
- The most common interview questions.
- How to answer every question.
- Questions that interviewers *cannot* ask.
- What questions *you* should ask your interviewer.
- What common mistakes you should avoid making.
- How to handle the post interview follow up.

I am absolutely certain that if you follow this guide you will greatly increase the chances of getting a teaching position. I strongly encourage you to print this out, mark it up as you see fit. In fact, you may want to bring it with to your next interview to brush up while you wait.

Where to Look for Teaching Jobs

I figured this would be the best place to start. Obviously, I will be unable to discuss *every* place to look for a teaching job since it will vary greatly from state to state. However, I will let you know of some of my favorite resources.

1. Networking:

This may seem obvious, but talking with other teachers and making connections is the best resource of all. In fact, I found out about the job at Springs School for one reason only: I was working as a student-teacher in the next town over. I made sure to ask everyone I met if they knew of any job openings *anywhere*. One day, that strategy panned out just right. I asked the right person and she told me that she thought the eighth grade social studies teacher at Springs School was going to retire at the end of the school year. Better yet, the retiring teacher had not yet made her retirement public. Therefore, the vast majority of my competition had no idea this job was going to open. I had a leg up on the competition before the game even started.

One strategy when networking is use the opportunity to conduct "Informational Interviews". In other words, don't open with "Do you have a job for me (if speaking with an Administrator)?" Or more generally "Do you know of any positions opening?" Most of the time contacts will not be able to say yes immediately which may end the conversation, or worse they may feel awkward not being able to help you and avoid further contact with you. Try opening with "Do you have time for a coffee to share some insights to what you see happening in education today?" Once you have the meeting and had some enriched conversation you lead into, "Where do you see opportunities?" And, most importantly, "Who else do you think I should speak with, and may I ask you to please make a warm introduction?" Always target to leave any informational interview with at least two new names — you will be amazed at how fast your network will grow!

> ** **Important Note:** Please do NOT underestimate the power of networking. There is a huge public misconception that teaching jobs are easy to find. Nothing in today's job market can be further from the truth! In fact, just getting an interview for a teaching position can often feel like a job in itself. Networking will not only help you find out what teaching jobs are available — it is the best, and often the only, way to actually get a job interview.

Social Media including Facebook, LinkedIn, and Twitter are powerful resources for networking. Technology is refining these social media tools all the time.

Here are some ways to use social media to land that job:

- Use social media to let people know you are job hunting! Whether through LinkedIn, Facebook, or Twitter, let contacts know the type of job you're looking for. They may not know of any jobs, but if they know you're looking, they'll think of you when one comes up. Enlist their help in checking popular job boards.

- Don't be shy about networking with your friends on Facebook! This medium—even though its original intent was not job hunting—can often prove more useful than LinkedIn. Your friends know you personally. They want to help. They want you to be successful. They are rooting for you.

- In this day of high tech, employers often check social media. Make sure the "you" that is being presented is the "you" which you want them to see. Check out and change your profile, photos. You might also consider changing some privacy settings to "friends only". More than one job has been lost or won on what is on your social media!

- Use social media to find out about the people who will be interviewing you. We'll talk later about using community and school websites to gain information about the school to which you are applying. Social media is a treasure trove of information about the people on the interview panel. LinkedIn profiles and Twitter feeds provide a wealth of information on individuals. Knowing more about those who are hiring for a job you want can help you adapt your cover letter, your resume, your interview study questions and answers to what they are looking for.

- Show prospective employers you have social media and technology savvy. Hyperlink your resume to Twitter and LinkedIn. This gives the employer another way to reach you. More importantly, it demonstrates your ability to interact online, and shows that you're social media-savvy. This is another way to show not tell about your techno-talents!

- Use those third-degree network contacts. Twitter is a great way to connect with others in your field who might not otherwise give you the time of day.

- If you have not already done so, create a complete LinkedIn profile. Become active on this network. This will help push your profile to the top of Google's search results—meaning potential employers will see what

15

you want them to see! Also the more you contribute the more people will see your perspective and refer others to you! Or at least endorse your abilities.

- Join chats on teaching. This helps you keep current on the latest concerns and innovations. Who knows? These chats could lead to network contacts and job prospects. Luck favors the prepared mind. Leave no stone unturned!

- Keep current on the latest social media tools. For example: Mention has replaced Google Chat in popularity. Mention is a great tool for identifying online mentions.

- Facebook provides endless possibilities to locate "friends" in the teaching and related fields who might be useful contacts.

- LinkedIn also works well for networking with people in your specific field. You can communicate with them via messages, invitations, introductions, and emails. Mentor endorsements can take you a long way in your field. LinkedIn is about connecting with people, finding and engaging people in mentor and other networking relationships.

2. College Campuses:

Any college that has an education department will have a website where they post teaching jobs. Let's face it, the college wants its students to get jobs. The more graduates who secure teaching positions, the better that college's teacher education program looks! At Southampton College, where I did my graduate work, I always made sure to check the bulletin board regularly for new postings. Actually, I did this even after I landed my job — just to see what else was out there.

** **Here's an important tip**: You do *not* have to attend the college to walk through their campus and have a look at their education department. While you're there, why not check out any potential jobs posted on their bulletin board?

** **Note:** The following suggestions are *state-specific*. Most states will have some way of checking for teaching jobs. However, those ways may vary greatly from state to state. For example: New York, and Florida (the two states in which I have taught) have very different methods of posting teaching jobs.

3. New York Teaching Jobs:

It's a well-known fact that, if you are looking for a job on Long Island, or anywhere in the New York Tri-State area, the best place to look is in the Sunday edition of the *New York Times* in the "Week in Review" section. The *New York Times* also has a very user-friendly website for doing job searches. Take a look at http://jobmarket.nytimes.com/jobs/category/education-training-jobs.

4. Specific state websites:

As I just mentioned, many states have their own website where you can search for teaching jobs. Do a Google search for "teaching jobs in {name of state}".

5. Local school district websites:

Don't just look at *state* websites. Many local school districts post jobs right on their own website as soon as something opens. For example: Manatee County in Florida uses the PATS system for searching and applying for jobs. It is easy to use. You simply register, look for jobs, and apply right online. Have a look for yourself: https://www.manateeschools.net/Page/6111

Of course, there is always the possibility that you are moving from one state to another or that you are interested in opportunities in several different states. If that is the case, I have a couple of websites I highly recommend:

K12JobSpot: www.k12jobspot.com:

This is a great *FREE* resource for anyone seeking a teaching job. You simply register for an account, put in the job(s)/state(s) you are interested in and K12jobspot.com will email you whenever there are jobs posted that match your description. Not only that, you will also get emails for upcoming job fairs in the states/counties that you are interested in. K12jobspot.com is definitely a great *FREE* service.

SchoolSpring.com: www.schoolspring.com:

SchoolSpring.com, is another *FREE* resource Subscribers have access to over 45,000 teaching jobs all for *FREE*. You can search by state, grade level, and job type.

Despite what many people say, teaching jobs can be very difficult to land—especially in certain parts of the country. Your best bet is to take advantage of *every* available resource.

6. The Internet:

Some websites which specialize in teaching jobs are listed below but Googling the terms 'teaching jobs' will obviously bring up more:

www.Teacherjobs.com

www.EducationAmerica.net

www.educationCanada.com

www.Jobsineducation.com

www.eteach.com

www.tes.co.uk

https://www.tes.com/en-us/

Apply To Education.com

www.applytoeducation.com/AttLogin.aspx

As Canada's premier paperless application system for school boards, *apply*to**education** streamlines the recruitment process for applicants by allowing them to fill out ONE application online and upload ALL of their supporting documents to complete their portfolio.

Education-jobs.co.uk

http://www.education-jobs.co.uk/

Education-jobs.co.uk is the UK's online job board that is dedicated to finding a job in the education sector. Jobs advertised cover the complete range from entry to senior level e.g. Teaching Assistants, Classroom Teachers, Head Teachers and Director/Principals to other as well as all other jobs specific to the education sector such as Educational Psychologists.

How to Get an Interview

Generally, when a school is hiring, the position must be posted. As mentioned earlier, this is usually done by means of a posting on an online job bank.

Getting an interview for the teaching position is not rocket science. However, the methods of achieving that interview vary from school to school. Therefore, it is best to know what the school's application process is before taking your first step.

There are four general methods of applying for a job. These include:

- sending a resume and job-specific application
- emailing your resume and job-specific application
- walking-in your resume and job-specific application
- applying online, following the application guidelines on the website

1. Sending a Resume

Many schools prefer that you mail in your resume. For this type of approach, it is best to include a cover letter AND a philosophy statement with your resume and job-specific application. The cover letter is a basic letter that describes the position that you are interested in and a few details about your qualifications and skills specific to the job for which you are applying. Your cover letter should convince the receiver that you KNOW what the job entails, you have the qualifications and related experience, and you are the BEST candidate for the job. If you don't accomplish this in your cover letter, the receiver will toss your application with the hundreds of others that did not make the cut and you will never get an interview.

The cover letter is basically your lead-in to your resume. Before writing your cover letter, you should know <u>exactly</u> to whom to address the letter. NEVER begin a cover letter with: "Dear Sir or Madame" or "To Whom It May Concern". It shows that you have not prepared and that you are not looking for a specific position within their school, but any job that you can get your hands on. Basically, it is disrespectful to your prospective employer. *(Cover letters will be discussed in much more detail later.)*

A philosophy statement <u>should </u>also be included with your cover letter and resume. This is a short (less than a page) statement about your beliefs about how students should learn. It is your own personal philosophy of education. I am always surprised at how many applicants do *not* include a philosophy statement with their resume and cover letter. Fortunately for you, that is a good thing! By submitting one, you will set yourself apart from the crowd.

See Appendix C: Sample Philosophy Statement.

2. Emailing Your Resume

Emailing is a common way for schools to receive resumes. More and more schools offer this method as an acceptable alternative. However, there are few tips concerning how to go about emailing your resume.

Attach your resume as a Word document or PDF file. These are the most common formats. PDF, or portable document file, has a more professional appearance.

Don't forget the subject line. The subject line should read like this: **Smith, John; 8th Grade Social Studies position**. This makes it easy for the recruiter to know who the email is from, and what it pertains to. It also assures that your email will be read. Also, it will help the Recruiter file the document.

Sometimes there are specific methods for addressing an emailed resume. Some schools have certain subject line requirements. If so, follow them EXACTLY!

3. Walk-In Your Resume

Schools may ask you to *walk-in* your resume because they want to get a look at your appearance right away. Or, you may to decide to walk-in your resume on your own hoping for a "chance" of meeting the principal. *This is something I strongly suggest.* It shows initiative, eagerness, and a willingness to go the extra mile to get noticed. It also allows you to get a feel for the tone of the school.

If you choose to walk-in your resume, you definitely want to dress appropriately. Basically, dress just like you would for an interview. Sometimes, a walk-in will result in an administrator giving you a brief interview on the spot to see if a formal interview will even be needed. So, definitely dress the part!

Sometimes, you will be requested to fill out an application form as well. Smile and be polite — no matter whom you are talking to. That could be the difference between getting an interview and just taking an extra trip for nothing.

Again, make sure to bring a cover letter, resume, and philosophy statement with you.

4. Online Application

More and more states and school districts require applications through an online process.

Florida is a perfect example. Most school districts in Florida and Ontario now require that you apply online.

If this is the case, make sure to follow their online application procedure correctly. In most cases, there will still be information you need to provide either by email, "snail-mail", or walk-in.

    ** **Important Note:** Just following the above procedures may not be enough to get the interview — even if you have done everything correctly. Many times, it takes a little something extra. Don't be afraid to take advantage of some of the contacts you have made or any other connections you may have. If you can get a job lead from a friend, ask that friend to give your resume and cover letter to the superintendent/principal. However, your contact/connection doesn't actually have to work at the school. Simply have your contact/connection place a phone call on your behalf anyway. A call from another teacher or fellow administrator can go a long way towards landing you an interview. When it comes to getting the interview, it can often come down to *whom you know*.

At Springs, we *always* gave interviews to applicants who had some type of connection/recommendation from a respected colleague. Now don't get me wrong! That does not mean that those people necessarily got the job. However, it did get their foot in the door for that interview.

In fact, that is precisely how I landed my first interview at Springs School when I was a student-teacher. I was very fortunate that my student-teaching supervisor at Southampton College was a very-well respected educator on the East End of Long Island. When he talked, people listened. When it looked like Springs School was in no rush to start their interviewing process for the job I wanted, I asked my supervisor if he could place a call over to Springs School (I already had another job offer and was going to have to take it if Springs didn't act.) The day after he called, I had an interview. The next day, I had the job.

Your Resume

With so many people searching for jobs these days, it is of the utmost importance that YOU make a great first impression.

In most cases, the only thing you have to create that first impression with is your resume. And, it is your resume and the accompanying cover letter that will get you the interview.

Here are tips on how to write a resume. These tips will help you create not just any resume, but a professional resume that clearly stands out amongst all the others. This resume will help you create that great first impression.

Format

When writing a resume use a professional resume format. There are several basic types of resumes used to apply for job openings. Depending on your personal circumstances, or the nature of the job for which you are applying choose from these resume formats:

- chronological
- functional
- combination
- targeted

The two most accepted resume formats today are chronological and functional.

Chronological Resume:

A chronological resume starts by listing your work history, with the most recent position listed first. Your jobs are listed in reverse chronological order with your current, or most recent job, first. Employers typically prefer this type of resume because it's easy to see what jobs you have held and when you have worked at them. Personally, I prefer chronological. From the interviewer standpoint I find it much easier to read and follow. A chronological resume format works best for those with a solid work (or volunteer) history. If your work experience is light — or nonexistent—you might profit from using a different format. Chronological resumes are generally easier to create.

Here is a sample so you can see what I mean:

Barret Smith, Junior
6 Napier Street
Stratford, Ontario N0R 1S0
519.555.5555 (home)
519.555.2222 (cell)
email:bsmith3@provider.com

EXPERIENCE

Key Holder

Add a brief overview of responsibilities.

The Loft Boutique April 2009—Present

Add a brief overview of the organization and scope of education/ services.

 ** Note:** *Some Human Resource personnel prefer to see the organization listed first then role, then results.*

Note the more objective the bullets are to highlight measurable results the better.

• Opened new specialty boutique that generated $XXXXX in revenue in the first year

- Place orders to restock merchandise and handled receiving of X products/SKUs
- Manage payroll, scheduling, reports, email, inventory, and maintain clientele book and records
- Integrated new register functions that improved customer cash-out by X%
- Extensive work with visual standards and merchandising high-ticket items

** **Note:** *Some Human Resource personnel prefer not to center everything. See above for an option*

Sales Associate,

Gucci — Collectors and Couture Departments July 2007—April 2009

- Merchandised designer women's wear
- Set-up trunk shows and attended clinics for new incoming fashion lines
- Worked with tailors and seamstresses for fittings
- Scheduled private shopping appointments with high-end customers

Bartender, **Bernie's Bar and Grill** February 2005—July 2007

- Provided customer service in fast-paced bar atmosphere
- Maintained and restocked inventory
- Administrative responsibilities included processing hour and tip information for payroll and closing register

Education: Bachelor of Arts, Western University, London, ON, 2012

COMPUTER SKILLS

- Experience with web design,
- teaching computer skills, night school, 2011 to present
- Presenter at Western University Kids and Computers Summer Camp, 2012–2013

Functional Resume:

A functional resume focuses on your skills and experience, rather than on your chronological work history. It is used most often by people who are changing careers or who have gaps in their employment history. Functional resumes are more time-consuming to prepare and require more thought and creativity. However, a functional resume allows you to demonstrate an understanding of the job for which you are applying and pick the skills you highlight to show how your experience, education, and skills make you an ideal candidate for a particular job.

Here is an example:

Olivia Hurst
336 Jackson Blvd. Elmira, NY 11111
Phone: 555-555-5555
Email: ohurst@aol.com

OBJECTIVE

To obtain a position where I can maximize my multilayer of management skills, quality assurance, program development, training experience, customer service and a successful track record in the Blood Banking care environment.

SUMMARY OF QUALIFICATIONS

(N.B. Use bullet points. Some Human Resource personnel will not read paragraphs of text. You need to make it easy to read quickly to get their attention. Othewise, it often gets filed away never to be looked at again! ☺)

- Results-oriented, high-energy, hands-on professional
- Successful record of accomplishments in the blood banking, training and communication transmission industries.
- Experience in phlebotomy, blood banking industry, training, quality assurance and customer service
- Focus on providing the recipient with the highest quality blood product, fully compliant with FDA cGMP, Code of Federal Regulations, AABB accreditation and California state laws.

27

Major strengths include

- Strong leadership,
- Excellent communication skills,
- Competent, strong team player,
- Attention to detail,
- Dutiful respect for compliance in all regulated environments and supervisory skills including hiring, termination, scheduling, training, payroll and other administrative tasks.
- Thorough knowledge of current manufacturing practices and a clear vision to accomplish the company goals. Computer and Internet literate.

PROFESSIONAL ACCOMPLISHMENTS

Program/Project Manager

Facilitated educational projects successfully over the past two years for Northern California blood centers, a FDA regulated manufacturing environment, as pertaining to cGMP, CFRs, CA state and American Association of Blood Bank (AABB) regulations and assure compliance with 22 organization quality systems.

Provided daily operational review/quality control of education accountability as it relates to imposed government regulatory requirements in a medical environment.

Assisted other team members in veni-punctures, donor reaction care and providing licensed staffing an extension in their duties by managing the blood services regulations documentation (BSD's) while assigned to the self-contained blood mobile unit (SCU).

Successfully supervised contract support for six AT&T Broadband systems located in the Bay Area. Provided customer intervention/resolution, training in telephony and customer care, Staff Scheduling, Quality Control, Payroll and special projects/ plant extensions and evaluations to ensure proper end-of-line and demarcation signal.

Reduced employee turnovers, introduced two-way communication to field employees, enhanced employee appearance and spearheaded the implementation of employee (health) benefits.

Chief point of contact for the AT&T telephone and the ABC Affiliated TV stations as it relates to complaints and diagnosing communicational problems either at the site or remote broadcasting. Also tested/repaired prototype equipment for possible consideration or for future use.

Reviewed FAA safety requirements and procedures to ensure compliance for aircraft and passenger safety.

Communication expert and programming specialist for the intermediate range Lance and Persian missile systems. Trained to operate and repair the (FDC) fire direction control computer system and field satellite communications.

Supervised and maintained the position of System Technician in charge of status monitoring and the integration of monitoring devices in nodes and power supplies. For the reception and transmission of telemetry to the network operation centers (NOC's) located in Denver, CO, and Fremont, CA. Designed plant extensions, improved the paper flow and inventory control for the warehouse. Provided preventative maintenance at the system level, face-to-face customer interaction when required and traveled to several telephony/@home systems in the U.S. for evaluation and suggestions in using the status monitoring equipment.

EDUCATION
- Associate of Art, Administration of Justice, San Jose University, San Jose, CA
- NCTI Certified, CATV System Technician, Denver, CO
- ABM Certified, Cornerstone Technician, Denver, CO

Combination Resume:

A combination resume uses the best of the above resume formats. It lists your skills and experience first. Your employment history is listed next. With this type of resume you can highlight the skills you have that are relevant to the job for which you are applying for while still providing an easy-to-scan chronological work history.

Here is a sample of a candidate applying for a job as a software engineer. Note how she tailors her work and education information to that job?

Jamie Black
225 North Terrace #8
St. Petersburg, FL 33716-2502
(727) 555-0191
jblack@provider.net

I am interested in pursuing a career in software development. I consider myself a fast learner and a team player. I feel that I can make a contribution to any Implementation Services department.

COMPUTER EXPERIENCE

Machines: IBM PC compatibles, Rockwell ACD, Macintosh

Languages: VBA, BASIC, Turbo Pascal, DB/c, Turbo C, COBOL

Programs: MS Access, MS Word, MS Excel, MS Outlook, Crystal Reports, MS Internet Explorer, Netscape Navigator, Support Magic, Norton Utilities

Operating Systems: MS 10, MS XP, MS Windows1, SCO UNIX, MS DOS

Hardware: Experienced with installation of mother boards, SIMM chips, internal/external modems, NICs, SCSI and IDE hard disks, SCSI floppy drives, SCSI I/O ports, and various printer configurations.

EXPERIENCE

1998 to Present Med Resorts International, Clearwater, FL

Systems Developer

Responsible for migration of extensive filePro database to MS Access utilizing tables, queries, forms, reports, macros, modules, and VBA. Troubleshoot and maintain existing MS Access database for Telemarketing Dept. Troubleshoot and diagnose UNIX, filePro, PC, and MS Windows related problems for in-house staff.

1995 to 1998 Lasergate Systems, Clearwater, FL

Support Engineer

Troubleshoot and debug minor program bugs. Modify existing programs with enhancements. Implement fixes and enhancements. Design, create, and implement ticket designs. Perform remote upgrades of ProtoBase and Select-a-Seat. Resolve problems and questions from Technical Support. Provide documentation. Assist Select-a-Seat Team Leader with creation and testing of new software.

PREVIOUS POSITIONS:

Senior Technical Support Representative

Technical Support Representative

Technical Support Operator

1988 to 1995 Home Shopping Network, St. Petersburg, FL

Help Desk Supervisor

Manage the Help Desk function as well as prioritizing, resolving, recognizing, and routing end-user computer problems. Establish and document policy and procedure.

PREVIOUS POSITIONS:

Help Desk Operator II

Assistant Data Systems Analyst

Telecommunications Systems Operator

Customer Service Phone Monitor Trainer

Customer Service Representative

Network Representative

EDUCATION

St. Petersburg Jr. College, St. Petersburg, FL
1986 to 1994
Major: A.S. Computer Programming and Analysis
GPA: 3.70
Warner Robins High School, Warner Robins, GA
1972 to 1975
Recipient of Who's Who in American High Schools

REFERENCES

Available upon request

Targeted Resume:

A targeted resume is customized so that it specifically highlights the experience and skills you have that are relevant to the job for which you are applying. It definitely takes more work. It's well worth the effort, especially when you are applying for jobs that are a perfect match for your qualifications and experience.

Here is an example:

Phoebe Walters
1121 Forte Circle, Toronto ON M5R 3B3
home: 416.555.1243
cell: 905.555.2222
email: pwaltersl@provider.ca

SUMMARY OF PROFESSIONAL QUALIFICATIONS

- Experienced manager with expertise in human relations and project management
- Extensive background in staff recruitment and retention
- Staff training and development
- Superb written and oral communication skills
- Organizational and Strategic Planning
- Management Coaching
- Program Marketing
- Contract negotiation and compliance
- Knowledge of Federal and State Employment Law

PROFESSIONAL AFFILIATIONS

- Society of Human Resources Management
- Portland Human Resources Management Association

PROFESSIONAL EXPERIENCE

CLINICAL DIRECTOR
Riverbend Inc., 2002–2012

- Senior Management of a Joint Commission on Accreditation of Healthcare Organizations (JCAHO) accredited treatment facility. Responsible for all aspects of program management; clinical, administrative, fiscal.

- Responsible for recruiting, orienting, training and supervising 50 staff, was able to reduce staff turnover from 68% to 14% by improving staff orientation and training, professional development, and mid-level management coaching.

- Oversight of all aspects of staff performance; performance evaluation, progressive discipline, mediation of staff disputes and grievance procedures in accordance with state and federal laws.

- Leadership in the setting and achieving of strategic and organizational goals.

- Established training programs for staff in regard to all aspects of workplace performance and professional development.

- Program Marketing, increased annual revenue by 38%.

PROGRAM DIRECTOR

R. Dykeman Center, 2000–2002

- Administrative, clinical, fiscal and human resources management of a large outpatient mental health center; 60 full time employees and 45 contract employees housed in various locations.

- Responsible for the recruitment and supervision and performance evaluation of clinical, administrative and medical staff.

- Provided training to enhance workplace performance at all levels of staffing.

- Nominated as Training Coordinator for the West Seattle Mental Health Consortium, providing training as the trainer or contracting with relevant professionals to provide training in the areas of culturally relevant services, professional ethics and law, and areas of professional development as requested by staff members.

- Concurrently completed a two-year certificate program in Organizational Development and Leadership as the recipient of a merit scholarship by the Microsoft Corporation.

- Independent Consultant to several small businesses, law firms, non-profit agencies and school districts on staff grievance procedures, team building and the setting and achieving of organizational goals.

PROGRAM DIRECTOR
Family Reconciliation Services, 1990–2000

- Provided program management of the largest FRS contract in Washington State.
- FRS was responsible for providing in-home crises counseling to families on a 24/7 basis.
- Responsible for the recruitment, orientation, supervision and performance evaluation of up to 45 Master's level clinicians.
- During this 10-year period, increased the ethnic diversity of staff from 0% to 36% and provided more culturally relevant services to the community served.
- Served as organizational and clinical consultant to a variety of organizations including Bellevue School District; Port S'klallam Tribal Health Board; Eastside Mental Health; Renton Area Youth & Family Services; as well as several businesses and law firms.
- Completed the training required to become an American Association of Marriage and Family Therapists (AAMFT) Approved Supervisor.

CLINICAL DIRECTOR – CHEMICAL DEPENDENCY TREATMENT PROGRAMS
Rogue Valley Medical Center, 1987–1990

- Hired by the medical center to design and implement a residential treatment program.
- Responsible for the recruitment and hiring of all staff; medical, administrative and clinical.
- Responsible for public relations and Program Marketing.
- Developed compensation structure and performance management and employee training and evaluation structures.
- Developed an on-going training program for nursing and clinical staff and served as a liaison between the hospital

and the community providing training to community partners; schools, the police department and relevant medical and mental health professionals.

- Designed and brought into existence a family education and support structure for the community.

EDUCATION

- Senior Professional Human Resources (SPHR) certification course work completed
- The Whidbey Institute, Organizational Development and Leadership
- University of Heidelberg, Germany, Psy.D in Clinical Psychology
- University of California at Berkeley, BA in Philosophy and German

---

2. Create your resume in the proper order using whichever format you deem most appropriate. Be sure to use correct spelling, grammar, and punctuation. Resumes with grammatical and/ or spelling errors go directly to the circular file (aka garbage). Word processor programs have spelling and grammar checks, but that is NOT enough! Print your resume and re-read the hard copy. Then ask a trusted friend or knowledgeable colleague read your resume as well. It is amazing what a fresh pairs of eyes can find!

3. Organize your resume properly under headings (such as education, skills, work experience, training, etc.) and put those headings in bold. When you work with the template of a specific resume format these headings are often set up for you.

Here are some good choices:

http://www.resume-now.com/lp/rnarsmsm31. aspx?cobrand=RSMN&tag=130928093015372& hitlogid=171609134&utm_source=GAD&utm_medi-um=SEMK&utm_campaign=Canada-1-9061

http://www.resumesolutions.ca/rs/
http://www.myperfectresume.com/lp/mprrwzlp06.
aspx?tag=130928093147899&hitlogid=171609373&co-
brand=CLEAR&tag=130928093147899&utm_
source=MPR&utm_medium=SEMK&utm_campaign=-
Canada-SEM-10428

4. Write your resume in such a way so that it matches YOUR skills and experience to the skills and experience needed for the available teaching position. This will make your resume look as if it was created solely or exclusively for this particular job rather than one generic resume you send out to everyone.

5. Use the jargon of the teaching profession in your resume. This gives the impression that you are a knowledgeable in your field.

6. Avoid using "I" in your resume. Make use of <u>action</u> verbs such as: collaborated, managed, established, created and adapted. A good resume uses both action verbs such as analyze, and achieve, and adjectives such as capable, resourceful, and experienced. As in the examples above make your accomplishments as objective as possible to show you can get results!

7. Make your resume presentable. Print your resume on high-quality resume paper. Use a laser printer. If you don't have one, print shops and stores such as Staples will print it. You may also want to dress up your resume to make it more distinctive. A nice border is an elegant way to make your resume stand out without being a distraction to the information within it. Don't go overboard. Professional — not cutesy — is the look you are seeking.

8. References, references, references! There are two schools of thought what to do with references. Some Human Resource personnel prefer the statement "References available upon

request. Others would prefer to list your references at the end of the resume with job title AND the phone number AND e-mail with each and every reference. You may also wish to include up to three letters of reference in your application package. If you are going to list references in your resume be sure to get the permission of the references first. It is recommended that you send them a copy of your resume.

9. When writing your resume objective, make sure to be as specific as possible. State the specific position you desire and one to two sentences to demonstrate why you would be the best candidate for that position. Use your objective to make your resume stand out amongst all the others. Look at the difference between these two examples...

   a. Objective: Seeking a Teaching Position

   b. Objective: Seeking an eighth grade social studies position where ten years of experience in teaching social studies can help [insert school name] meet and exceed state standards.

See the difference?

10. Be specific with the rest of your resume as well. Far too many resumes are filled with generalizations. This is not a good way to show your experience and skills. Instead, your resume should contain relevant information for the specific teaching position.

   ** **Note:** Make sure you are prepared to clearly explain *every skill and experience* on your resume. Administrators often use your resume as the basis for their interview questions!

11. Add information on your resume like your hobbies. That is the first place Human Resource personnel look because it often tells them more about you as a person. It is stuff that you do on your free time that gives insight to them about

you (e.g. violin, reading vs. captain of hockey team, family camping gives a very different perspective and view about you to fit their role expectations)

Of course, there are also quite a few things that administrators *hate* to see on resumes as well. Many people do not think that administrators or interview committees really go all the way through a resume, but they really do. Many have certain pet peeves when it comes to reading a resume. Based on my experience with reading hundreds of resumes, I've included a list of things that you should avoid when putting your resume together.

- Omitting vital information. You absolutely need to show all of your important pertinent information without making people search for it. If you are applying for a teaching job it is not pertinent that you have a degree from Cordon Bleu — unless this will be an asset for the job you are seeking.

- Do NOT put down every job you've ever had.

   ** **Note:** It's advisable to leave out older stuff 15+ years out — see comments below about gaps.

Unrelated experience is not necessary and can actually distract the reader. Being selective shows you know the job. However, don't rule out hobbies or related experience that may be an asset. For example: If you are applying for a job as a physical education teacher and you have CPR certification and Red Cross Bronze Leader Patrol accreditation in swimming, these are pertinent skills. A teacher I knew once was deemed the ideal candidate because she had served as the editor for the Teachers' Union Strike Newsletter during a six-week teachers' strike. The school needed someone to be staff advisor to the school's yearbook committee. Who knew?

- Major gaps in your employment history leave an administrator wondering about your work ethic. Be prepared to answer questions if you have such gaps.

** **Note:** Pay attention to the above advice. Although it's best to leave out irrelevant experience, it may leave the impression of a gap in your employment. This may cause administrators to screen you out too early for this reason! Summaries that are hard to follow and understand are annoying. Keep any summary easy, organized, and brief.

- Fancy fonts and colors are nothing more than a distraction. Use easy-to-read, simple, plain fonts like Times Roman or Calibri. Be consistent. Use ONE font throughout your cover letter and resume. You can vary font size and make use of bold or italics for emphasis.

- Avoid writing your resume as a narrative or in the first or third person. It is irritating to read and comes off as arrogant. Stick to a standard resume format!

- Pictures and/or graphics on a resume are also distracting and unnecessary. Avoid them.

- Needlessly adding objectives and introductions on your resume is boring. Administrators know what your objective is ☺. However, as I noted earlier, if done right, you *can* make your objective help you stand out from the crowd.

- Including false or misleading information on your resume is a major mistake. There are always ways for a recruiter to check up on you. Many do, so don't lie! Getting caught in a lie on a resume tells a prospective employer that you can't be trusted. Your resume will automatically end up in that circular file and your name will be black flagged for any future employment opportunities with the employer.

- Sending a resume that doesn't exactly match the type of job that you are applying for is extremely irritating. You are wasting everyone's time. This also shows you do not understand the requirements of this job or you are too lazy to custom tailor your resume. Either is a bad first impression.

- Using overly long paragraphs in a resume makes it harder for the recruiter to read and makes the task take too long. Use bullets of information.

- Resumes that are more than two pages are much less likely to be fully read by anyone. That's just reality. If you can make your resume one page with a second page of references information that is ideal. That said, don't make the font size smaller than 12 point just to cram a lot onto a page. Recruiters aren't getting any younger and they do not appreciate straining their eyes to read hundreds of resumes.

- Dating the information in your work history in the wrong order makes your resume harder to follow. Work history should always be listed chronologically, with most current jobs at the top.

- Spelling and grammatical errors prove that you are not very keen on details. Your resume — no matter how impressive — will be rejected based on these errors!

If you're still struggling with your resume I strongly recommend Jimmy Sweeney's Amazing Resume Creator. With this software you can create a professional looking resume in just 10 minutes! Click here for more information:

http://teaching.amazresume.hop.clickbank.net/

Your Cover Letter

A cover letter is: *A letter sent with, and explaining the contents of, another document or a parcel of goods.* Its main purpose is to highlight the skills, experience and education which make you an ideal candidate for the job. The cover letter indicates the specific job for which you are applying, where and when you saw this job advertised. It closes with a request for an interview cleverly worded.

Creating the perfect cover letter does not have to be difficult. Cover letters are generally short and to the point.

However, what most people don't realize is that your cover letter is NOT supposed to get you the job. The sole purpose of the cover letter is to get you <u>noticed</u>!

Therefore, in many cases the cover letter may actually be more important than the resume!

It is becoming more and more difficult to get a teaching position. Retirements in most North American districts have not kept up with declining enrolment. Only two Ontario school districts have growing populations in elementary and secondary school enrolments.

And, more and more people are changing careers and looking to the teaching profession as a more fulfilling career and lifestyle choice. Lawyers, accountants, computer programmers, police officers have begun to move to teaching careers in secondary and college positions.

Plain and simple: There is no shortage of teachers!

In fact, just getting an interview for a teaching position is extremely difficult.

So, what does this have to do with your cover letter?

Everything!

Now more than ever you need to make your cover letter stand out.

The biggest mistake teachers make when writing their cover letter is not starting out with a BANG! Grab the readers' attention from the first sentence!

While teachers teach their students all the time how important it is to think about their audience when writing, teachers seem to forget this when it comes to writing their own cover letters.

Teachers should think about who is going to read the cover letter, when they are going to read, and why are they going to keep reading.

Your cover letter will most likely be read by an administrator and/or an interview committee that has been put in place.

These people are very busy!

They will most likely be reading stacks of cover letters at a time...possibly as many as a hundred at a time.

Now, if you were ever to sit down and read 100 cover letters in one sitting you would notice something very quickly...cover letter after cover letter would simply start to blend into each other.

This is because most teacher cover letters start off with a typical boring opening line such as, "I am writing in response to the ad in the New York Times about a teaching position at blah, blah, blah."

What you need to do if you want to move onto the next step in the hiring process is make your teacher cover letter STAND OUT!

Remember, the cover letter is not about getting the job. The cover letter is about getting you noticed and one step closer to the interview. A great way to achieve this goal is by actually putting an attention grabbing headline at the top of the cover letter such as, "Three reasons why I believe I am the best candidate for the teaching position at ...". Then, following this headline, you start you cover letter with, "Dear Mr. Jones."

Believe me, this will get you noticed and will have a much better effect than dull teacher cover letters that never get a second glance.

However, if this is too drastic an approach for you then you may be able to achieve this goal in a more subtle way by simply starting your cover letter with something other than "I am writing in response to the ad in the ..."

Whichever approach you choose, subtle or drastic, you need to make sure YOUR teacher cover letter stands out from the pack and starting out with a bang by grabbing the reader's attention is the best approach. However, in my experience, most teachers do not do this and that is a big mistake.

Just as with your resume, there are things to avoid in your cover letter so that it and the attached resume do not end up in that dreaded circular file.

The quality of your cover letter will determine the employer's first impression of you. The following are general guidelines to help you design your cover letter.

- Use a business letter format.
- Keep the letter limited to one page, using paper identical to the paper used for your resume.

- Address the letter to an individual by name, correct title, organization and exact address. If you do not have a specific name, you can also address the letter to a "Selection Committee".

- Highlight your skills and abilities that are relevant to the position you are seeking. Go beyond a restatement of what's already on your resume. You want to convince the selection committee that you know the job and you have the skills and experience to do this job outstandingly!

- Tailor the letter to the specific position and organization.

- Focus on the needs of the employer, and how you can fulfill them! Provide proof from your experience.

- Be positive and professional in context, tone, word choice, and expectations.

- Include a closing statement that expresses your positive intentions on being interviewed, hearing from that individual and/or taking the next step. This statement brings closure to the letter and shows you are motivated to meet with the committee and discuss how you are an excellent candidate for this job.

- Carefully spellcheck and proofread. Get someone you trust to read it over.

Below is an example of a cover letter that would have been acceptable just a couple of years ago. Today, it will never get you to the interview stage!

****

July 4, 2006
RE: The 8th Grade Social Studies position that is available.
Mr. Brown
3232 Jackson St.
Jackson City, FA 32443
Dear Mr. Brown,

I am writing this letter in regards to the 8th Grade Social Studies position that has recently become available at [School Name]. As my enclosed resume will show you, I have three years' experience as a Middle School Social Studies teacher at [Your School and Location].

My philosophy of education is based on a student-centered classroom in which I use a variety of teaching techniques to meet the students various learning styles. Therefore, students are active participants rather than passive learners. In addition, I hold my students, as well as myself, to the highest of expectations.

As a future member of the [Name of County or Town] community, I would appreciate an opportunity to meet with you to discuss my philosophy of education and the possibility of filling the vacant secondary social studies position. Teaching in [Name of County or Town] would be a great opportunity for me and my family.

I thank you for your time and look forward to hearing from you once you have had the chance to read my resume.

Respectfully,
YOUR NAME
Enclosure (2)

****

Below is an example of a cover letter that stands out.

TIP **Pay attention to the** format **of this cover letter.**

*****START LETTER*****

September 28, 2019
{NAME}, {TITLE}
{SCHOOL}
{ADDRESS}
{CITY, ST ZIP}
Dear {NAME}:

I have a strong desire to interview for a teaching position with (state school or district name. Your (school or district is my top choice of places I'd like to teach. I would love the opportunity to interview in person for a teaching position at (name district or school). Thank you in advance for your consideration.

Over the years I have had the opportunity to hold some extraordinary teaching and training positions. I am now looking forward to applying my extensive knowledge, skills and experience with {SCHOOL} for a permanent full-time teaching position.

- Exceptionally well qualified in the management of differentiated classroom — particularly with difficult/problem students.
- Passionate for igniting student curiosity and self-learning for the Social Sciences — especially in current events and the political process; Certified in Social Studies 6-12.
- Experienced in adult education and in teaching English, Life Skills, Math, Reading, and Science at the high school and middle school levels; Certified in Middle Grades Integrated Curriculum 5-9.

I hope you'll agree that the combination of my qualifications and experience for this position are a perfect fit as you will see from the enclosed resume.

I am excited about the possibility of a personal interview at your earliest convenience to further discuss my credentials with you.

Sincerely,

{NAME handwritten}
Name Typed
Enclosure: Resume

*****END LETTER*****

I know it is difficult for some teachers to accept this style and approach to writing a teacher cover letter, but hopefully it will at least get you to think a little differently about that traditional, somewhat dull, cover letter.

Once Your Cover Letter is Written

So now what?

Once your cover letter is written what do you with it? I know what you're thinking… *"Should I just send it in with my resume?"*

Well, if that's all you're going to do, you are certainly not going to stand out above the competition — which can be very tough when it comes to getting a teaching job.

So, what should you do with your cover letter?

Well, first of all, you are not just going to *send* in your cover letter and resume. Instead, you should *walk* in your cover letter and resume.

That's right! You are going to *hand-deliver* your cover letter and resume. When you do this, it will put a face to the name and will most definitely make you stand out from all of those other applicants who merely mailed or e-mailed theirs in.

However, more important than "standing out" is the fact that an administrator may actually give you an interview on the spot! So, dress as if you were going for an interview!

The second thing you're going to do is write three versions of your teacher cover letter.

That's right! Three versions. You need to stop thinking of your cover letter as just one individual letter and more as a series of three letters.

The first letter is the traditional cover letter. The one we just discussed that you both send in AND hand-deliver that are both accompanied by your resume.

It's the second and third cover letter, however, that are going to really separate yourself from the crowd.

Remember, the old *Head & Shoulders* commercial slogan? *"You only get one chance to make a first impression."*

Well…maybe that's not entirely true. Maybe you get *two* chances:

Your second cover letter is known as a "follow-up cover letter". This cover letter comes AFTER you have landed the interview, but BEFORE the actual interview takes place. In those few days in between, you send out your "follow-up cover letter".

This cover letter is similar to your original cover letter with some minor changes. Your follow-up cover letter is "slightly" less formal. It is somewhat of a cross between a cover letter and a thank you note.

Start the letter off with a thank you for the upcoming interview at [insert date and time]. Make sure you include the date and time. This will make you stand out even more…*they* will be looking forward to *your* interview!

Once you have thanked the appropriate person, highlight the key points you made in your original cover letter.

The third in the series of cover letters is the "post-interview cover letter".

This third "cover letter" is much less formal and is leaning more towards a thank you note than a cover letter. In fact, this third letter should actually be presented as a "hand-written" note on nice, professionally monogrammed stationary.

You give this third letter to <u>each and every person</u> that sat on that interview committee. Address each by name and keep it short. Start by thanking the person for his/her time AND make sure to add something specific from your interview. This will again, make YOUR interview stand out. Next, wrap up that letter with something specific about their school and your passion to teach there.

But wait! You're not done!

Make sure you...***Don't Give Up!***

If your "post-interview cover letter" doesn't get you a phone call within a couple of days, then follow-up with an email...

If that doesn't work, then follow-up again with a phone call.

Persistence can pay off big time and can be the difference between getting a teaching job and being back to looking for more interviews. Be politely persistent!

This cover letter process is extremely powerful. It will put you light years ahead of the competition.

Here are the steps once again:

1. Original Cover Letter ~ mail AND hand-deliver along with resume.

2. Follow-Up Cover Letter ~ mail AFTER you get the interview, but BEFORE the interview takes place.

3. Post-Interview Cover Letter ~ hand-written thank you, less formal, on nice stationery, follow-up email, and follow-up phone call. *(There will be much more on the post-interview follow up later)*

Plain and simple: You greatly increase your chances of getting a teaching job when you use this approach.

Remember, the role of the cover letter has changed dramatically over the course of the last couple of years. Don't make the mistake of writing the same old boring cover letter as everyone else.

Today the cover letter is an extremely important tool! Don't take this too lightly.

Preparing for the Interview

Once you get the call for the interview, the next thing that you have to do is prepare, prepare, prepare. You can never over prepare! The more prepared you are, the less likely you will be to make mistakes. Giving a great interview is not as hard as some may think, but only *if* you are prepared. Here are a few things you need to do to prepare for your next interview:

Remember, during an interview, you are a salesman. You are there to sell yourself to your prospective employer. You want to market yourself in the most interesting way possible. Great preparation for the interview is your best bet. A salesman that is knowledgeable, friendly, and positive always gets the deal.

Do Your Research

It doesn't matter how much knowledge or experience you have about the teaching position you are trying to get if you don't have a clue about the school itself. It is simply disastrous to enter into an interview and not be able to tell your interviewers what *their* school is all about. How else are you going to tell them why you would be an excellent addition to their staff?

Get to know about a school by reading its website. You can get a great deal of general knowledge about a school that way, including the names of key people and their job titles. (There will be more on that in a minute.) Sift through their website, including the pages that show samples of their work, such as lesson plans, curriculum maps, etc.

Another thing that would be nice to do is to check out the surrounding area. It looks very good during the interview if you can make a comment about a particular school's community. This is especially important when community members are included on the interview committees as is often the case.

Another way to get a little extra information about the school is to simply call them on the phone and ask general questions without necessarily referring to yourself as a potential employee. You can call as someone who is interested in moving to the area. While this is a little less than forthright, it does glean some great information.

Real estate offices in the school area are often treasure troves of information. Don't be afraid to tap this resource. Who knows? You might even end up buying a home in this community.

Look for school events to attend. This allows you to rub elbows with staff and parents. Upcoming events will be listed on the school's website.

Find a friend. Through social media, it isn't hard to find a friend of a friend — a staff member who is willing to talk about the school.

Know Your Contact

When called for an interview, ask with whom you will be interviewing. It is nice to be able to greet your interviewer by name at the beginning of the interview without first being told who they are. It shows that you are on top of things, and have prepared beforehand. In most cases, you will be interviewed by a committee, a panel of three to five people. This panel can be a mix of administrators, teachers, board members, and/or community members. If you can find out specifically who is on the panel, you are in much better shape to establish a bond during the interview and to have a greater level of comfort during the interview.

Do as much research on the person, or people, conducting your interview as you can. Learn what they do for the school/community. I was very impressed when a particular candidate I was interviewing made reference to one of my websites. Big Bonus Points! ☺

If you know the grade level that you are going to work in, you may want to get the names of your potential colleagues and administrators prior to the interview. This way, you can get some information about their roles in the school and their teaching styles.

Mention some of the things you learned about your potential colleagues in the interview and about how much you look forward to working with them in the future. If you can, give an example of their work (lesson plan, website, article etc.) so that you will appear more sincere and informed.

Practice Your Responses

It is best, especially if you are prone to nervousness, to practice giving your responses to the most common interview questions. (A list of the most common questions will appear later in the book.) You should also practice your wording, the tone of your voice, and body language. Your responses should always be as specific and detailed as possible. You do *not* want your answers to be too general or too brief.

While you are practicing your responses, you will also want to practice ridding yourself of any odd habits you may have, such as expressing yourself with your hands or biting your nails.

Practice your answers first in front of a mirror. Memorize what you are going to say but not to the point of reciting answers.

You need to appear relaxed and attentive even if those butterflies are flying around in your stomach!

When you are comfortable with your answers, it's a good idea to practice answering your interview questions with a friend. Get his or her opinion about your delivery and gestures. Perhaps your friend will have some nice insights for you to use during the real interview.

Video a mock interview with a trusted colleague or mentor. This time the "interviewer" should ask you the questions you have prepared BUT also add some of his own where you have to formulate answers on the spur of the moment. The more you anticipate questions, the less you will have to deal with these "surprises".

Dress the Part

Pre-select your attire the day before your interview. You want to make sure that your clothes do not have any wrinkles or stains on them. Pick an outfit that best suits the position for which you are applying. Again, a little research by visiting a school's website, or better yet, visiting the school itself, will give you a good idea of how teachers dress at that school. However, remember, you are putting your best foot forward. It is always better to overdress than under dress.

Of course, if you are planning to work as a physical education teacher or even an art teacher, you can usually dress a little more casually. Just be certain to avoid wearing denim jeans, oversized clothing, and undersized clothing. Women should try and avoid wearing too much make-up.

Even in the hotter seasons, you should *never* wear sandals or gym shoes to an interview. It sends an unprofessional message. The same goes for hats and other accessories.

Get Organized

Make sure that all of the things that you will need for the interview are prepared the day before. I strongly suggest that you make a checklist of important items you don't want to forget.

Here is a list:

- Several resumes (*Be prepared to discuss anything on your resume.*)

- Copy of your teaching certification

- Letters of recommendation

- Copy of driver's license and social security card (*you never know* ☺)

- Copy of criminal reference check—if you have already had one done. Chances are if you've worked with kids or volunteered for organizations that work with kids, you already have one.

- Sample Lesson Plans (*Lesson plans should cover a wide variety of topics and teaching styles — that way you can refer directly to actual lessons when asked about various teaching methods you use .*)

- Examples of student work (*Have examples of student work that go with the sample lesson plans.*)

- Picture books I use in class (*These may also go with the sample lessons.*)

- UBS flashdrive version of any published and/or unpublished writing you've done on teaching strategies (*If you are involved in any extra curricula activities that are related to teaching then bring in what you can. My plan was to always leave an interviewer with a copy of my book: Become an Effective Teacher in Minutes: Best Teaching Practices You Can Use Now* as well as my eBook: 52 Teaching Tips*)*

- If you are working with kids, in class or as a volunteer, get someone to record a lesson and create a video. Leave a copy on a flashdrive with the interview team.

- Notepad/pen *(Have a list of questions you want to ask written down. We'll get that later.)*

How Should I Act?

The truth of the matter is a successful interview is not *all* in the words that come out of your mouth, but often has a lot to do with your mannerisms. Statistics show that interviewers are not just wondering if you are skilled enough for the job, they are often wondering if you would fit in nicely with your co-workers. Your personality is a big part of your interview and can make all the difference. You obviously do not want to be chewing gum or breath mints during your interview and you also don't want to speak in slang during your interview either. It is unprofessional and rude.

Here are some more things that you should pay particularly close attention to during an interview:

Make a good first impression.

Research shows the first thirty seconds of an interview are often make-or-break time! First impressions can leave lasting impressions in people's minds and this is often intensified in job interviews.

Psychologists have shown that people weigh initial information much more heavily than later information when they evaluate people. It's a simple fact: The first information people get about anything — a person, a place, an idea — influences the way they process later information. In other words, people are more likely to believe that the first things they learn are the truth!

What's involved in this first impression? Body language! Make sure your body language as you enter the interview projects a professional image.

Make good eye contact. This conveys confidence and eagerness.

Smile naturally. Enter the room with a friendly, energetic expression. Let the interviewers know you are glad to be there and looking forward to their questions.

Maintain good posture as you enter the room and throughout the interview. Sit up straight, relax, cross your feet at your ankles or place feet firmly on the ground, don't slouch and don't rock back in your chair.

Ditch the gum before you enter the room!

Show Confidence

You MUST enter that interview with an attitude of success. You cannot mope or exude too much placidity in your manner. It is not inviting, and does not give the impression of a person that anyone wants to face on a daily basis, especially students.

Be sure of your abilities without appearing arrogant. You want to let your interviewer know that you are fully prepared to excel at your job, without alienating other teachers. You should point out your accomplishments in your field while remaining somewhat humble. A good idea is to list your accomplishments in a matter of fact way.

When it comes to showing confidence, you need to understand that body language plays a large part. Practice good posture, sit straight, keep your head up, and keep eye contact.

Keep a Positive Attitude

You should always try to smile and keep a positive outlook during your interview. If you hear something that doesn't sound good to you, don't frown and look disgruntled, just keep a slight smile on your face until it is time for you to say something. Then approach your interviewer with your questions or concerns when the time is appropriate.

Maintain Eye Contact

Keeping eye contact with your person asking the question(s) at an interview is very important. Keep your eyes on the interviewer who asked the question but sweep your gaze to include the other members of the interview panel. Each should feel you are talking directly to him/her. DO NOT look around the room or at the items on the interviewer's desk. This makes you seem distracted, disinterested, or just plain snoop. Just imagine what you would be thinking if you were interviewing someone and he was looking all over the room!

Body Language

We've touched on this a little bit, but you should keep in mind some of the common errors that many people make when they are speaking to others. I've listed some of the common things that you should avoid during an interview.

1. Avoid fidgeting while speaking to your interviewer. It shows a lack of self-confidence. It is also distracting for the interviewer(s).

2. Avoid using overly expressive hand gestures. It is distracting.

3. Avoid biting your lips in between sentences. It gives the impression that you are making things up.

4. Do not sit with your arms crossed because it is a closed body posture. Aim for open, inviting body language.

5. Do not shrug your shoulders when asked a question that you are unsure of. Instead, take a second to think of your

response. Shrugging your shoulders gives the impression that you don't know the answer. It is unprofessional.

6. Don't answer with nods and headshakes. Use words to answer questions.

7. Get plenty of sleep the night before the interview. You don't want to yawn in front of the interviewer. He will think that you are expressing boredom.

8. Do NOT bite you nails, play with your hair, twiddle a pencil or use any of those irritating habits!

9. Make sure your palms are dry. Use a firm—not crushing—handshake and repeat the name of the interviewer as you shake his/her hand.

Some final pre-interview advice?

Check out the route to the building and the exact room in which you will be meeting a few days beforehand.

Know exactly how long it takes to arrive.

Get there EARLY!! You do not need the stress of worrying about time. Arriving early creates a good first impression. Sometimes interviews are actually running ahead or someone has cancelled and the panel might be ready for you earlier.

What Administrators are Looking for

In order to have a leg up on the competition, it is important to understand what the interviewers are evaluating you on during an interview, so here is a helpful list:

- **Your Enthusiasm**: Administrators want to know that you are willing and eager to be a part of their school. Being fully stocked with knowledge about their school is a sure fire way to show your enthusiasm.

I tell people all the time… "I can teach someone *how* to teach, but I *cannot* teach someone how to be enthusiastic." You can't teach passion. You either have it or you don't!

- **Your Ability to Speak Clearly**: If you approach an interview mumbling or speaking slang, a prospective employer will not see you as a professional or someone he would want interacting with his children daily.

- **Your Teamwork Skills**: You should show or describe an example of your ability to work as a team during your interview. If you can build in reference to the members of the school team with whom you would be working this will impress the interviewers that you have done your research.

- **Leadership Skills**: You should show your leadership abilities by approaching your interview with a confident not cocky attitude. If you get an opportunity to discuss examples of your leadership skills be ready with descriptive yet succinct examples.

- **Problem Solving Ability**: Administrators need to know that you can handle yourself when a problem arrives. That's why they may ask you a strange question or ask how you would react in a hypothetical situation. Be prepared to show that you can problem solve effectively.

- **Work-related Experience**: You definitely want to show that you have some experience in the position you are applying for so that the administrator knows that you will not be overwhelmed. This might include teaching experience and/or volunteer work. If you get a chance to volunteer at the school where the job is posted, it is an excellent strategy and research opportunity!

- **Community Involvement**: Employers love to see that you have done volunteer work. It shows that you take pride in your community, and have a willingness to be a team player.

- **Knowledge of the School:** Again, administrators like to see that you have done your research about their school. It shows that your interest in working for them is sincere. Volunteering at the school is an excellent idea.

- **Flexibility**: Administrators want to know that you are able to go with the flow. It proves that they can depend on you later. Have a good example ready.

- **Ambition and Motivation**: Ambitious people are generally motivated enough to make great improvements in the school. Ambition usually means more success for the school. Be prepared to show where you have shown initiative.

- **People Skills:** Your ability to get along with others is very important to an administrator. They need to know that you won't ruffle any feathers when you are hired. Having some understanding of the staff through volunteering, supply teaching or doing some fact finding before the interview give you a step up at the interview.

- **Professional Appearance:** Nobody wants a slob working in their school. Be certain to dress appropriately for the teaching position that you are applying for. When in doubt, overdress rather than underdress. A simple suit with clean lines and a good fit is always safe. Make sure your shoes are shined!

- **Ability to Multitask:** This is a very necessary skill in teaching. Every day you will be required to do several things at once. Be prepared with a good example to demonstrate this skill.

- **Computer Literacy:** The ability to work a computer is important. It is best to keep up with the most common software like MS Office and and apps for productivity and creativity.

- **Reliability:** Administrators want dependable and reliable people to work for them. Your ability to arrive on time and well prepared for the interview is a good place to start ☺.

- **Knowledge of Content:** You absolutely must convey a superior knowledge of the content you intend to teach. Anything less is simply unacceptable.

- **Knowledge of Teaching Strategies:** You must also let your interviewers know that you use the most effective teaching strategies to address various learning styles, increase standardized test scores, get 100% class participation, and limit classroom management problems.

If you are looking for an arsenal of effective teaching strategies I strongly recommend that you read *Become an Effective Teacher in Minutes: Best Teaching Practices You Can Use Now* and *How to Succeed as an Elementary Teacher*.

Administrators are also monitoring and evaluating you on three basic skill sets during an interview. Those three skill sets can be broken down into these sections:

Content Skills

These are the skills that are directly related to teaching a specific content area. If you are lacking in certain content areas, you can simply express that you are looking into taking classes or professional development courses in that area. It may not be exactly what the employer is looking for, but it shows that you show initiative.

Functional Skills

These are the skills that reflect your ability to work with others. This is where an employer decides whether or not you are a team player. You can display this skill by displaying your past employment record and accomplishments that are directly job related.

Generally, an employer will get an idea of your ability to work with others depending on your reasons for leaving previous jobs, whether or not your were denied tenure before etc. If you have been denied tenure before, don't lie about it, and do not act bitter about it when discussing the reason, this will not benefit you in the end. Be forthcoming and sincere. Express that it was a learning experience for you and tell them what you learned from it. It reflects well on your temperament.

Adaptive Skills

This is a general show of your personality and temperament. It also covers your self-management skills. During your interview, the interviewer will be evaluating you on your general ability to get along with him/her. Your general personality traits are monitored during this time.

When faced with a difficult question, you do not want to get defensive or angry. Just take a few seconds to think about what you should say rather than say something you will regret.

You want to appear at ease (as much so as you can) during your interview. You want the employer to think that you anticipated everything that he/she is going to say. Even if you are terrified...*never let them see you sweat!*

Your First Impression

"You only get one chance to make a first impression"

— Head & Shoulders Commercial

First impressions can be a hard thing to get past in any situation. During an interview you want to give the best first impression that you can. There are many small things that you can do to assure that you give the best first impression possible.

Here are some tips:

- You can never be too polite to the secretary, or the person that directs you to your waiting area when waiting to be interviewed. A small gesture such as asking, "how are you doing" can work wonders for you when you leave the building later.

- While waiting to be interviewed, sit properly and behave as if everyone passing by is your potential interviewer (they just might be). Smile at people as much as possible. Do not act impatient or bored, it sends the wrong message. Some interviewers will keep you waiting just to see how you handle yourself.

- Greet you interviewer with a firm handshake, a smile, and a, "Hello Mr./Mrs. *Smith*"

- Remain standing until your interviewer asks you to be seated. It is simply polite and shows proper etiquette.

Again, dress according to the type of teaching position that you are applying for.

- Show yourself to be well organized, by having all things needed for the interview.

- While waiting, do *not* eat or drink anything. And, don't bite your nails!!

- Definitely do *not* chat on your cell phone while waiting for your interviewer. It makes you look distracted. And, of course, absolutely make sure your cell phone is OFF...not "vibrate"! OFF!!!

Dos and Don'ts

As someone who has witnessed many simple mistakes during the interview process I share this basic list of the dos and don'ts during an interview.

Dos	Don'ts
Arrive on time, or better yet, 10 minutes early.	Be overly aggressive or egotistical.
Refer to the interviewer by name.	Spend interview time talking about money. Your research should already have answered money questions.
Smile and use a firm—not crushing—handshake.	Act disinterested or uninformed about the school community.
Be alert and act interested throughout.	Act defensively when questioned about anything.
Maintain eye contact at all times.	Speak badly about past colleagues or employers.
Make all comments in a positive manner.	Answer with only *yes* or *no or merely nod or shake your head*.
Speak clearly, firmly, and with authority but not with aggression.	Make excuses, lie or hide facts about your work history.
Accept any refreshment offered if you are not too nervous to cause a distraction with this. I usually politely decline. There are too many ways this can go badly.	Ask for coffee or refreshments.

Common Interview Questions

Every interview consists of a several questions. Many of these are standard questions. I've listed the most common questions that you will encounter during an interview to help you get a handle on them and prepare well thought out answers.

By knowing the most likely questions *before* the interview starts, you will have a major advantage on the competition. Knowing the questions will allow you to prepare your answers beforehand so that you don't get stumped.

Let's face it, while I cannot possibly predict *every* question that is going to be asked, there are certain questions that will *definitely* be asked AND there is a right and wrong way to answer these questions.

> ** **IMPORTANT NOTE:** Answering questions with generalizations, rather than specifics, will guarantee you DO <u>NOT</u> GET THE JOB! Your answers <u>MUST</u> be specific and you <u>MUST</u> use examples from actual lessons to support your answers...*This is the key to acing any teacher interview.* Have a few strong examples ready and rehearsed that clearly demonstrate your strengths and ability to get results. Weave them into an answer even if not explicitly asked — remember you are selling YOU!

Below, I've included tips on how to answer the questions AND actual sample answers.

Example answers are specific to middle school social studies. It would be impossible to provide sample answers for every grade level and every subject area. This is where your research and your ability to be specific come in!

To prove that you are the best person for the job, you need to take these sample answers and adapt them to your specific grade level and content area.

After reading a handful of sample answers, you will start to see a pattern. You will quickly understand what I mean when I say: *You MUST use examples from actual lessons to support your answers.*

Be warned: Some of these answers may seem lengthy. Remember: *You* want to be the one controlling the interview.

> ** **Important Tip:** The more you know about your interviewers the more you can base *your* answers on *their* interests. For example, if you are a U.S. History teacher you can easily use examples from lessons on a wide variety of topics including the Harlem Renaissance, Women's Rights, the Holocaust, Japanese Internment. Wherever possible, you want to choose your answers based on who your interviewers are.

Most Common Interview Questions, Tips, and Sample Answers:

1. Tell me something about yourself.

Tips:

- Always say something positive.

- Your reply should show that you have both experience in the area you are applying and a wealth of varied life experiences.

Sample Answer:

After graduating with a degree in political science, I moved out west to pursue my love of the outdoors, particularly skiing. I spent five years learning how to ski in the backcountry with the use avalanche beacons and other safety equipment. During my years in Colorado, I worked my way up through the restaurant business and became the kitchen manager at an upscale Italian restaurant. My life experiences in Colorado were invaluable. While skiing the backcountry, I learned that I could do anything that I put my mind to. I learned how to set goals and reach those goals through hard work and practice. Through my restaurant experience, I learned the importance of working as a team, how to be a leader, and how to multi-task. I moved back to Long Island because of my father's health. After being out of the mountains for a short time, I realized that the restaurant business was not for me. I decided to go back to school to obtain a masters' degree in elementary education. I have been very fortunate in my education career. I have had excellent professors as well as a fantastic associate teachers...

I could go on, but I assume you get the idea. At the time of my first interview at Springs School I had significantly more "life experience" than I did "teaching experience". I used my life experiences to show my strengths (responsibility, leadership, team-work, and multi-tasking...) even for a question as simple as, "Tell me something about yourself."

2. How do you handle stressful situations?

Tips:

* Obviously, answers to this question will vary depending on who you are and how you actually handle stress. However, this is a common question as teaching is definitely a stressful job. Your best bet is to say something that that shows you handle stress in a *constructive* way.

Sample Answer:

When I exercise regularly, I am able to handle stressful situations better. I also make sure to be well-prepared and well-organized for all my lessons to reduce the stress that may arise.

3. **Why do you think that you would be a good fit with this school?**

Tips:

- This is where your research comes in handy!! Use information you discovered from your research of the school to explain why you would be a good fit.

- Think about some of the things you are interested in that you know the school excels in. For example, their technology program. If a school's website mentions they have a TV production lab, I always make sure to mention my experience coordinating the eighth grade video editing team and how I would love to get involved with their TV production lab.

- Make sure to comment about the community...when I applied for my first teaching job at Springs School I told the interviewers that I was a member of the Springs community and that my son was going to be attending Springs School and therefore they were stuck with me one way or another.

- If you have experience, make sure to use this open-ended question to push your strong points. For example, *Not only have I been teaching eighth grade social studies for five years, but I have also taken on a leadership role in our school. I have been the eighth grade advisor for the past three years. My responsibilities include planning and conducting the eighth grade trip and running the eighth grade graduation ceremony. I also became a teacher mentor responsible for training new staff members and presenting workshops on effective teaching strategies.*

- You may also want to say something like this...*Since your school is very well respected, I assume you have*

*many applicants for the position. Therefore, you have
the luxury of being somewhat choosy…I would assume
you are looking for someone that is more than just well
versed in effective teaching strategies, but someone
that brings something extra…I believe that I bring that
something extra to the classroom and to the school.*

4. Have you ever been fired/denied tenure, and why?

<u>Tips:</u>

- Well, the best answer would obviously be "No".
However, you definitely do *not* want to lie about this.
And, do not blame the situation on someone else. If
you have been denied tenure for any reason simply be
honest with your interviewer and let him know that it
was a learning experience for you.

5. Where do you see yourself in 5 years? 10 years? 20 years?

<u>Tips:</u>

- There are obviously many ways you can answer this
question. Here are a couple of suggestions…*I love being
in the classroom so I plan on being in the classroom for
the next twenty years. However, I will also continue to
learn and improve my teaching throughout my career as
well as help other teachers improve.*

- Here's another…*After teaching for the next ten years, I
am planning on pursuing an administrative degree so I
can work with curriculum development.*

Notice that while both answers were very different they
also had something in common. Both answers imply that the
person being interviewed intends on growing professionally
as an educator.

6. Do you prefer to work on your own or as a team?

Tips:

- Obviously, you must answer with "team". Nobody wants to hire someone who is not a team player. However, this is a great example of a question where it is vitally important that you pull out examples from actual lessons.

Sample Answer:

Definitely I am a team player. Teachers are always the best resource for other teachers. I think being a team player is essential to being a good teacher. At my current school, the teachers work closely together and all contribute to scheduling, discipline, school wide events and other activities. We also often do team teaching activities. For example, I worked closely with the language arts department during our recent World War II unit (be specific). We coordinated our curriculum so the students were reading novels such as Night and I Have Lived a Thousand Years at the same time as they were learning about the Holocaust in their social studies class. We also opened up the wall between the two rooms and combined the classes for a week-long project on the impact that World War II had on the home front. Students worked in groups of five to create a newscast on how one particular group of Americans was impacted by the war. The students did the research, wrote scripts, created posters, and presented their newscast combining skills and content learned in both language arts and social studies.

Notice how specific I was. The interviewers learned a lot more than whether or not I like to work as a team. The interviewers learned about a great unit that the students at *their* school would get to be a part of if I became their new teacher!

7. Why are you interested in working for this school?

Tips:

- Again, this is where your research comes in handy. Maybe you came across something during your research of the school that you would like to be a part of. Administrators love it when a candidate knows something about their school and has a good, honest reason for wanting to work there.

- When I applied to Haile Middle School I talked about how my wife and I fell in love with the Bradenton area when vacationing in Florida and that we were looking to buy a home and raise our family close to the school.

- My response when I was applying to Springs School several years earlier was quite similar…

Sample Answer:

I have been a member of the Springs community for the past three years and have decided to raise my family here. My son will be going to this school and it would be a great opportunity for me, and my family, if I was to work here…

8. What is your philosophy of education?

Tips:

- It is important that your philosophy of education matches the school's. Otherwise you will both be unhappy. However, do not lie. Do not tell them simply what you think they want to hear. As a teacher you must know what your philosophy of education is and you must be able to stand by that philosophy. Look at how your philosophy and the school's mission statement are compatible. The interview panel will be impressed with your research and your thinking through this.

- Make sure to have a written copy of your *philosophy statement*. In fact, I would include a copy of your philosophy statement along with your cover letter and resume with your original application package. But you should also make sure to bring extra copies with you to the interview.

Here are two different examples:

Sample #1 *My Philosophy Statement on Education*

I believe that each child is a unique individual who needs a secure, caring, and stimulating atmosphere in which to grow and mature emotionally, intellectually, physically, and socially. It is my desire as an educator to help students meet their fullest potential in these areas by providing an environment that is safe, supports risk-taking, and invites a sharing of ideas. There are three elements that I believe are conducive to establishing such an environment, (1) the teacher acting as a guide, (2) allowing the child's natural curiosity to direct his/her learning, and (3) promoting respect for all things and all people.

When the teacher's role is to guide, providing access to information rather than acting as the primary source of information, the students' search for knowledge is met as they learn to find answers to their questions. For students to construct knowledge, they need the opportunity to discover for themselves and practice skills in authentic situations. Providing students access to hands-on activities and allowing adequate time and space to use materials that reinforce the lesson being studied creates an opportunity for individual discovery and construction of knowledge to occur.

Equally important to self-discovery is having the opportunity to study things that are meaningful and relevant to one's life and interests. Developing a curriculum around student interests fosters intrinsic motivation and stimulates the passion to learn. One way to take learning in a direction relevant to student interest is to invite student dialogue about the lessons and units of study. Given the opportunity for input, students generate ideas and set goals that make for much richer activities than I could have created or imagined myself. When students have ownership in the curriculum, they are motivated to work hard and master the skills necessary to reach their goals.

Helping students to develop a deep love and respect for themselves, others, and their environment occurs through an open sharing of ideas and a judicious approach to discipline. When the voice of each student is heard, and environment evolves where students feel free to express themselves. Class meetings are one way to encourage such dialogue. I believe children have greater respect for their teachers, their peers, and the lessons presented when they feel safe and sure of what is expected of them. In setting fair and consistent rules initially and stating the importance of every activity, students are shown respect for their presence and time. In turn they learn to respect themselves, others, and their environment.

For myself, teaching provides an opportunity for continual learning and growth. One of my hopes as an educator is to instill a love of learning in my students, as I share my own passion for learning with them. I feel there is a need for compassionate, strong, and dedicated individuals who are excited about working with children. In our competitive society it is important for students to not only receive a solid education, but to work with someone who is aware of and sensitive to their individual needs. I am such a person and will always strive to be the best educator that I can be.

Sample #2 *Philosophy Statement*

I believe the children are our future…

I believe each and every child has the potential to bring something unique and special to the world. I will help children to develop their potential by believing in them as capable individuals. I will assist children in discovering who they are, so they can express their own opinions and nurture their own ideas. I have a vision of a world where people learn to respect, accept, and embrace the differences between us, as the core of what makes life so fascinating.

Teach them well and let them lead the way…

Every classroom presents a unique community of learners that varies not only in abilities, but also in learning styles. My role as a teacher is to give children the tools with which to cultivate their own gardens of knowledge. To accomplish this goal, I will teach to the needs of each child so that all learners can feel capable and successful. I will present curriculum that involves the interests of the children and makes learning relevant to life. I will incorporate themes, integrated units, projects, group work, individual work, and hands-on learning in order to make children active learners. Finally, I will tie learning into the world community to help children become caring and active members of society.

Show them all the beauty they possess inside. Give them a sense of pride…

My classroom will be a caring, safe, and equitable environment where each child can blossom and grow. I will allow children to become responsible members of our classroom community by using strategies such as class meetings, positive discipline, and democratic principles. In showing children how to become responsible for themselves as well as their own learning, I am giving them the tools to become successful in life, to believe in themselves, and to love themselves.

Let the children's laughter remind us how we used to be... Teaching is a lifelong learning process of learning about new philosophies and new strategies, learning from the parents and community, learning from colleagues, and especially learning from the children. Children have taught me to open my mind and my heart to the joys, the innocence, and the diversity of ideas in the world. Because of this, I will never forget how to smile with the new, cherish the old, and laugh with the children.

<u>Sample Answer:</u>

My philosophy of education is based on a student centered classroom in which the teacher acts more as a guide in the learning process. My philosophy is heavily based on the idea that all students are actively involved throughout the entire lesson. I believe that by keeping students actively involved in all your lessons you will greatly reduce classroom management problems, increase class participation, and improve standardized test scores. I make it point to move away from the teacher centered, textbook driven curriculum to a more constructivist approach and I make sure to use a variety of teaching methods to meet the students various learning needs. For example, I use simple strategies such as the "all-write" strategy, the pair/share strategy, and checking-for-understanding to keep students involved. I will also use cooperative jigsaws so the students are not only constructing their own knowledge, but also teaching other students (give example here)...I also believe it is important to address higher order thinking skills...I often tell students that what makes social studies such a great subject is that there are not always right and wrong answers, but rather it is how you make an argument and support that argument that is important...

For example, as a closure activity for a lesson on the use of the atomic bomb to end World War II, I have the students make an argument on whether or not they think President Truman made the right decision and students must support that argument with specific examples from the day's lesson. Certainly, there are arguments that can be made either supporting or condemning Truman's decision…neither argument is right or wrong. What is important is that the students can make that argument on their own AND support that argument with facts. In this way students are not just learning about the important event in history, but they are also using higher order thinking skills.

Again, notice how I used examples from actual lessons. If you do this enough you will leave the interview with your potential employees feeling completely confident that you know what you are doing!

9. How do you incorporate technology into the classroom?

Tips:

- You must stress that you firmly believe technology should play a big role in today's educational system. However, you must also stress that using technology in the classroom goes beyond the teacher using Power Point presentations. Rather, technology should be integrated in a way in which the students are the ones learning how to use it properly.

You must explain how the use of technology is beneficial to the students. In other words, how you use technology to improve academic achievement.

Sample Answer:

Technology in the classroom plays a big role in today's education system. Teachers have many advantages today that we simply did not have that long ago. It is important that teachers take advantage of these new technologies to increase student motivation and improve academic achievement. For example: web quests are great way to spark student interest in a topic. At the start of my unit of the "Roaring Twenties" I have students do a web quest called "a walking tour of Harlem" as a motivational activity and introduction to the Harlem Renaissance. Students get to see and read about the many artistic events of the era and, even better, they get to listen to the Jazz music of the time.

However, I must say, that in today's world it is critical that teachers go beyond simply using technology as a teaching tool. What teachers need to do is to teach their students how to use technology. My favorite way to incorporate technology is to do activities in which students learn both content AND computer skills. For example, during our unit on "Colonial Life" students worked in pairs to research and create a brochure on one of the thirteen original colonies. Students not only learned a great deal of content, in a fun way, but they also learned how to search the internet for quality information, copy and paste pictures into a network folder, and combine everything into a beautiful brochure using Microsoft Publisher. (Of course, at this point, I would obviously pass around several examples of the brochures that the students created).

(I could also continue with this if it appears that the interviewers like what they hear...)

I do a similar project with the Civil War in which students work in groups of five to create a Civil War newspaper, again using Microsoft Publisher. Each student has a different article to write for their newspaper so there is an individual piece as well as a group piece.

10. How do you handle classroom management issues?

Tips:

- This is an *extremely* important question. Without a doubt, you will be asked this question!! Your answer could be the difference between getting the job and not getting the job. In fact, I am always shocked at how many people get this answer poorly.

- Make sure to explain that classroom management is *not* about rewards and punishments, but rather it is about keeping your students actively involved in all of your lessons…that you are *proactive* as opposed to *reactive.*

- Also, this question may be asked in a more specific manner with the interviewer actually providing a hypothetical situation and asking you how you would handle that particular situation.

Sample Answer:

The best "classroom management plan" is a strong "instructional plan". In other words, I do not use an elaborate system of rewards and punishments to address classroom management issues. Instead I find it much more effective to be proactive. You see, the vast majority of classroom management issues arise for two reasons: 1) boredom; 2) confusion.

Addressing both of these issues starts from the second the students enter the classroom. By keeping students actively involved throughout the lesson the students will not get bored. I do this through simple teaching strategies such as the "all-write" and the "pair & share".

For example, instead of asking a question and having the same handful of students respond by raising their hands, I'll ask a question (give a specific example here) and tell all my students, "You have 3 minutes to write down an answer..."

After their three-minute time limit is up, I will then tell all students to take two more minutes to discuss their answer with their partner or group. In this way I have taken what would have been less than 10% class participation and turned it into 100% class participation. And, those students who would have raised their hands anyway, have now had a chance to develop stronger answers.

Another way I keep all students actively involved is through the use of cooperative jigsaws.

If you are unfamiliar with cooperative jigsaws or are looking for creative group activities I strongly recommend you read my book Become an Effective Teacher in Minutes: Best Teaching Practices You Can Use Now Jigsaws are a great way to turn an otherwise dull lesson into an exciting student centered activity. For example, when teaching the "Causes of the Industrial Revolution", instead of giving the students the five major causes and having them memorize the information, the students were split into five "expert groups". Each expert group was given information on one particular cause with a graphic organizer to complete. After roughly 10–15 minutes of reading and completing their organizer as a group, new groups were formed with each new group containing an "expert" on one of the five causes...

All of these activities keep the students actively involved and therefore reduce boredom and therefore limit the opportunity for classroom management issues to arise in the first place.

However, that only addresses the boredom issue. The other reason classroom management issues arise has to do with student confusion. Therefore, it is important for teachers to anticipate and clear up any possible confusion about what the students are to do. For example, I always have my day's agenda and, most importantly, the lesson's objective, clearly posted. And, I make absolutely certain to go through both at the beginning of every class. I do not think these things should be surprise to your students. And of course, I also check-for-understanding often throughout the lesson by simply having a student repeat the directions back to me.

11. How do you integrate curriculum across subject/content areas?

Tips:

- This is another *important* question. It is also another *opened-ended* question that will allow you to go ahead and run away with the answer. In other words, not only is it easy to answer, but it should be easy pull specific examples from actual lessons.

Sample Answer:

Integrating curriculum is an essential element of teaching because it addresses how people learn. In "real life" we do not learn things in isolated vacuums. Also, integrating curriculum allows teachers to address their number one enemy: Time.

My entire social studies curriculum is integrated with language arts. In my class my students are writing formal essays, creative stories, dialogues, and poetry. Students are reading historical fiction and non-fiction, as well reading both primary and secondary sources. And, students are giving presentations that address not only content, but public speaking. In fact, you would be hard pressed to find anything that is done in a language arts class that is not done in my social studies class. The only difference is that I teach these skills revolving around specific historical content.

Sometimes I do this within my own classroom and other times it is in conjunction with the language arts department. For example, one of my all time favorite lessons is on Japanese Internment. I introduce the topic by reading a picture book to my students entitled So Far from the Sea.

(I would actually bring the picture book with me to the interview so at this point I could show it to them!)

Following a discussion of the book, students analyze a series of oil paintings created by Japanese-Americans placed in internment camps during World War II and complete a graphic organizer based on each painting. They then use their completed graphic organizers to create a haiku from the perspective of a Japanese-American interned in the United States during World War II.

(Of course, I would show my interviewers actual examples of haikus that the students created. Nothing is more powerful than examples of student work! For privacy reasons, remove names of students)

However, I also work together with the language arts department in which we actually open up the wall between our classrooms and combine our classes for a complete interdisciplinary unit. For example, in a unit on the U.S. "home front" during World War II, students from both classes are placed in mixed-ability groups and each group creates their own 5-minute newscast on one particular group of Americans that were impacted on the home front during World War II (African-Americans, women, children, Mexican-Americans, Japanese-Americans, consumers etc.). Groups are responsible for writing a script, creating a poster, and presenting their newscast to the rest of the class.

In this way we are integrating skills and content from language arts and social studies.

12. How do you increase student motivation to learn?

Tips:

- Make sure to stress the connection between student motivation and academic achievement and let them know that you are well versed in many ways to increase student motivation to learn. As always…be specific!

Sample Answer:

Increasing student motivation is essential to increasing academic achievement. I find that the best way to do this is by making connections between what the students are learning and what is going on in their own lives…in other words, what is important to them. With social studies this is fairly easy. For example, in our unit on the "Roaring Twenties" I have students read an expert from the Great Gatsby that discusses "flappers", but before they read I have all the students make a list of things that today's youth does that may be considered rebellious. After the students have generated their lists and shared them with their partners we then discuss the connections between today's youth and the flappers of the 1920s with their short bobbed hair, short skirts, and their crazy Charleston dance. Of course, when I show the students the pictures of what was considered "short skirts" in the 1920s, they are totally surprised.

The bottom line is: If you can get the students to "want" to learn then everything else becomes much easier.

Another way teachers can go about increasing motivation to learn is with simple critical thinking questions. For example: in the lesson I mentioned earlier on Japanese-Internment, I actually start off with a critical thinking question asking the students if they think the President has the right, during times of war, to violate individuals rights in order to protect national security. This usually turns into a heated discussion and it is at this point that I introduce the topic of Japanese-Internment. The students are then eager to learn what F.D.R did and whether or not it was the right thing to do.

(Again, I could go on and on. What you need to do is be able to "read" your interviewers and know when to keep going and when to stop. It is better to stop after one or two examples and ask if the interview panel wants you to go elaborate further than to have them wishing you would shut up!)

13. How do you increase parent involvement?

<u>Tips:</u>

- This is a tricky question because, let's face it, parents can be a teacher's best friend or a teacher's worst enemy. Nevertheless, you must convey that you are aware of how important parental involvement is AND that you have a plan *in place* to keep parents informed and involved in their child's education.

- Letting your interviewers know that you plan to call all of your student's parents during the first few weeks of school just to touch base is a great start.

- Having some type of website and/or blog that will keep parents up-to-date is also very impressive. Posting homework assignments so parents are aware of upcoming tests or projects is also an excellent strategy.

<u>Sample Answer:</u>

Obviously, parents play a crucial role in the education of their kids. They "can" and "should" be a great asset to teachers. We share the same goals, after all. Unfortunately, as we know, this is not always the case. However, there are some simple ways teachers can improve parental involvement. First of all, the first contact with parents should always be positive. So I make sure to contact all of my parents during the first few weeks of school just to touch base and introduce myself. This takes a little bit of time, but it pays off in the long run. Especially, when you need to call a parent with some unpleasant news later in the year.

Another way I keep parents informed and involved is with my blog. Last year I set up my own homework blog to help both students and parents. At the beginning of every week I make a new post on my blog. I start by giving a brief overview of what we will be doing for the week and then I list the homework assignments for each day of the week. In fact, whenever possible, I even scan in copies of worksheets so parents can print them out from home.

But here's the best part...Parents sign up on my blog for automatic updates. What this means is that every time I update my blog, which is at least once per week, all my parents automatically get sent an email with a link to the new post. The feedback from the parents has been highly favorable. As you can imagine, it has greatly improved the amount of homework and studying that gets done.

14. What is your homework philosophy?

Tips:

- Homework should *never* be used to teach new material.

- Homework should be a relatively short assignment that reinforces what has *already* been taught. Often "homework" is what is not completed in class by the more methodical students. Quicker students seldom have homework beyond studying or preparing for an upcoming assignment by doing some pre-reading.

- Emphasize the fact that homework can be a great tool to help improve student's academic achievement, but only if done right.

Sample Answer:

Sometimes I think homework is one of the most misunderstood concepts in education. There is definitely a right way and a wrong way to assign homework. First of all, let me make this perfectly clear: I never assign homework to teach kids "new" material. As I like to say, "This is not a correspondence course ." My homework assignments are designed to reinforce something that we have already learned, either in that day's lesson or in lesson's from previous days, or a combination of both. Or, homework is a pre-reading assignment so students are ready of the new lesson or concept the following day.

Now, with that said, there are two obvious problems that teachers face with homework. One: getting the students to actually complete the homework, and two, getting the students to complete the homework without cheating.

There are couple things teachers can do to overcome these obstacles. As far as getting kids to complete their homework, I make sure to save the last couple of minutes of each class to get the homework started in class, not completed, but just started. This does two things: First, it clears up any questions the students might have about how to do the homework. Second, it eliminates the "I didn't know we had homework" response.

As for the kids cheating? This is a big issue. However, it can be avoided if teachers give homework assignments that go beyond simple question and answer. I find that short writing assignments work best. For example: During a recent lesson on immigration I had students write a journal entry as if they were an immigrant at the turn of the century. Their journal could be as creative as they wanted, but it must include terms and facts learned from that day's lesson, such as the date, the country they came from, and various "push-pull factors" that led them to come to America.

Another quick example would be something I do after presentations. I simply have students create their own five-to-ten-question quiz based on the presentations that were given in class that day. I may even have students exchange quizzes at the beginning of the next class for further review.

While I realize it is difficult to completely eliminate cheating on homework, the examples I just gave make it much more difficult than the typical short answer or multiple choice homework assignments.

15. Give me some examples of projects or hands-on activities you use in your classroom.

Tips:

- Your potential employer wants to know that you are not going to simply lecture to your students. They want to see that you use a variety of activities including different types of projects or hands-on activities. This is another great question that you *want* to be asked because it allows you to go into detail about one of your great lessons or units.

- Make sure that if the question is asked in different way, such as, "Do you enjoy doing hands-on activities?" you don't just say, "Yes," and stop there. Make sure you also explain *why* you think it is important and give at least one specific example.

** **Note:** You may begin to notice something interesting during the interview ☺. What you'll notice is the interviewers will begin their questions with, "I was going to ask you (such-n-such), but you already addressed that with an earlier answer."

You see, when you answer interview questions by giving examples from actual lessons you may be addressing many other *potential* questions that the interviewers are *planning* to ask. For example, the lesson that I teach on Japanese-Internment during World War II addresses multiple intelligences, integrating curriculum, increasing motivation to learn, the use art and poetry in the classroom. Therefore, if I use that example in one of my answers I may very likely be addressing something someone else was going to ask like language across the curriculum.

Don't worry. If you hear someone during the interview say these words, "I was going to ask you this but…" it is a good thing. It means that you are the one controlling the interview and that is exactly as it should be.

Sample Answer:

I try to do at least one major project each quarter and those projects can take anywhere from one to three weeks—depending on what is involved. But in the end, I always find that the time it takes to complete a successful project is definitely worthwhile.

Most of my projects are a combination of research, writing a script or dialogue, creating a poster, and finally presenting the skit to the class. These are usually done in a "jig-saw" format so that each presentation is teaching another part of the "puzzle".

For example, one of my favorite projects is what I call the "Civil War Interviews". I divide the class into 12–15 pairs depending on class size. Each pair then receives a different person from the Civil War era such as Abraham Lincoln, Jefferson Davis, Robert E. Lee, Frederick Douglas etc. Students then research their person and create a dialogue for a television series entitled "Timeline". It is fictional show in which the host of the show has a time machine and travels through time interviewing famous people from the past. Once the students have done their research and created their scripts they then create a poster for their person and rehearse their lines for the presentation. The final presentations are also filmed to give it more of a television studio atmosphere (plus their fun to watch). Following all the presentations students are tested on all people presented during the "Civil War Interviews".

I enjoy doing these types of projects because it teaches the content, addresses various learning styles and various intelligences, but most importantly, it does all this in fun way. The kids really enjoy it.

My book, *Become an Effective Teacher in Minutes: Best Teaching Practices You Can Use Now,* has an entire chapter devoted to projects and gives a step-by-step explanation of how to set-up five of my favorite projects. For more information go to any online bookstore.

16. How do you address different learning styles/multiple intelligences?

Tips:

- Most administrators today want to know that you are well versed in Howard Gardner's theory of *multiple intelligences*. If you are not, do a quick Google search for "Howard Gardner". You will be able to do your own research. The basic principle is that there are many different types of intelligences (7–9 the last time I checked!). Unfortunately, most schools usually teach to only one or two of these intelligences.

- What you need to do in your interview is convince your potential employers that your lessons address a variety of intelligences and learning styles.

- This is where you want to give examples of how you use art, music, video, writing, speaking, hands-on projects, and activities that involve the students actually moving about the room.

- Of course, as I stated earlier, if you are answering the questions correctly (by providing *specific* examples from *actual* lessons) then this question may already have been addressed and may never come up. Look at the sample answers I have provided thus far. Many of them already address Gardner's theory of multiple intelligences.

Here are examples from different grades and subject levels:

SUBJECT AREA: Seventh grade science

Students will increase their knowledge of the botanical world.

Students will be able to apply scientific techniques to different areas of study.

Students will able to identify and classify trees from their communities by using many different teaching strategies.

INTELLIGENCE: Verbal/Linguistic Intelligence

Students will be assigned to a specific tree, where they will be responsible for creating an identity for that tree. Individually, they will give the tree personal traits and characteristics in a short essay format.

INTELIGENCE: Logical/Mathematical Intelligence

Students will count the rings on a tree in order to calculate the tree's approximate age.

In groups of two, students will calculate the age of a tree by counting the number of rings that appears on a tree stump.

INTELLIGENCE: Spatial/Visual/Verbal and Interpersonal Intelligences.

Students will describe to partners what a tree looks like.

Using partners, one student will vividly describe the visual aspects of a specific tree to his/her partner, while the other will visualize it in his/her mind. Upon verbal description, the student will then draw the tree to see if their visualizations match the description of the other student.

INTELLIGENCE: Musical/Rhythmic/Auditory Intelligences

Students will learn and memorize 20 different types of trees from a specific area.

Using rhyme, rhythm or song, small groups of students will identify and name specific trees in any type of format that they may wish to use.

INTELLIGENCE: Bodily/Kinesthetic and Intrapersonal Intelligences

Students will feel and describe a tree.

Individually, students will choose a tree that is somehow appealing to them. He/she will touch and carefully examine that tree, and then in a journal describe what it feels like and explain what impression it leaves them with.

INTELLIGENCE: Junior Grade Health Class

Students will understand the general health of our society.

Students will be able to understand nutritional intake in order to promote healthy choices in the course of their lives.

1. Students will be able to effectively read nutrition labels on food products.

2. Students will explore their own nutritional intake and habits.

3. Students will formulate an advertisement to educate others concerning health and nutrition.

4. Students will compare the nutritional labels of different products.

5. Students will explore the different types of advertisement in order to sell a product.

INTELLIGENCE: Logical/Mathematical:

After learning how to interpret the labels on food products, students will practice calculating percentage of fat, sodium, cholesterol, etc. in terms of daily intake.

INTELLIGENCE: Bodily/Kinesthetic:

Students will visit the local grocery store and compare/contrast the nutrition labels of the same food distributed by different companies (Oscar Meyer vs. Ballpark hot dogs). They will document which product they would select as a consumer.

INTELLIGENCE: Spatial/Visual:

Students will divide into small groups (interpersonal) and create a new product that may increase that health of consumers. Students must consider daily intake and nutritional health concern when developing the new product. They will use large poster board to create a billboard or commercial advertisement. They also have the option of presenting this portion of the assignment in the form of a video-recorded commercial advertisement.

INTELLIGENCE: Musical/Rhythmic:

The students will create a jingle for their new product. The jingle must incorporate health issues and nutrition.

INTELLIGENCE: Verbal/Linguistic:

Students will create a brief newspaper advertisement to sell the new product. Again, the product should attract people who are concerned about health and encourage others to become conscious of health.

INTELLIGENCE: Interpersonal:

Each group will present the new product to the rest of the class and gather input regarding if the class believes that the product would sell considering the nutritional information and the advertising methods.

INTELLIGENCE: Intrapersonal:

Students will keep a journal of their own nutritional intake and determine if it follows the average nutritional consumption.

17. Take me through a typical lesson.

Tips:

- I had an administrator who *always* asked this question. What he wanted to get was a visual image of how your class is looked and sounded.

- Make sure to specifically explain how you *open* and *close* your lesson.

Sample Answer:

When the students enter the room, they will see three things on the board every day: the "do now" assignment, the day's agenda, and the lesson's objective. As soon as the students enter the room they get started on the "do now" assignment. This works as a great way to reduce classroom management problems, review older material, or even use as a springboard into new material.

Following the "do now" I always make sure to go through the day's agenda and, most importantly, the lesson's objective. I basically say something like this, "Today we are going to be learning about the Panama Canal. We'll start off with a short video clip that is about 7-minutes long. After that, we will work in pairs to complete some map work on the region. Then, we will do a short reading assignment on the Panama Canal. We'll wrap it up by starting a letter to President Roosevelt that you will finish for homework." The whole time I explain the agenda I am also pointing to the board where it is written. I then move onto the objective in the same manner, "By the end of class today you will be able to define key terms such as "isthmus" and "Latin America", you will be able to explain how the United States acquired the isthmus of Panama, and you will be able to argue what type of foreign policy you think Roosevelt was using and whether or not you agree with his decisions." (Notice the higher order thinking skills).

Because I make the agenda and objective perfectly clear, the students are not surprised. I'm a firm believer that what you want the kids to learn should not be a surprise to them.

After discussing the day's objective, I then take the majority of the remainder of class and divide it into mini-lessons—maybe three ten-minute activities or two fifteen-minute activities. For example, the lesson I did on the Panama Canal was broken into a 10-minute video clip and discussion, followed by ten minutes of map work, and then a ten-minute reading activity. In this way students are never really getting bored.

I then make sure to save at least a few minutes at the end of the lesson for a closure activity/homework assignment. For example: following the reading assignment in the Panama Canal lesson, students receive their homework assignment which is to write a letter to Theodore Roosevelt about his foreign policy involving the construction of the Panama Canal. Students can either agree or disagree with President Roosevelt, but they must back up their argument with specific details from the day's lesson.

18. Describe how you would set up your classroom.

Tips:

- Interviewers may ask this question because they want to have some type of visual image of what your room will looks like.

- While this seems like a simple question, you can still use it to plug some of the strategies you use as a teacher. For example, discussing how you arrange your desks will also give you the opportunity to discuss how you use different types of group work.

- Do not make the mistake of saying you have examples of student work up all over the room. Too much displaying of student work can actually be distracting.

Sample Answer:

I actually put a lot of thought into how my room is set up, particularly the walls. I am not the type of teacher that has student work up all over the classroom. I have found that too much student work can actually be distracting, especially in the front of the room. Instead, I keep the front of the room very simple. My front wall will have the "do now", agenda, and objective written on it everyday in the same exact location. The only other thing I have up front is a bulletin board that clearly states the unit we are currently studying and includes pictures and primary sources from that time period. There is not much else in the front of the room other than any notes I may need the students to copy down. Personally, I have always found it quite distracting to enter a room with the front board covered with gibberish.

On the side walls of the classroom is where I put student work and inspirational quotes.

And, the back wall is where I save things for me. You see, the back wall is the wall that I look at the most so I use that space to leave myself reminders. For example, I always have 3–5 teaching strategies written on the back wall that I know I need to work on. This is very effective, because it catches my eye and I say, "Oh yeah…" I also keep the bell schedule written on the back wall as well as any other information that I might need such as any students who need to make up work, class pictures etc.

Now, as for the desk arrangement, it is rarely the same two days in a row. I arrange my desks before the lesson starts based on what activity we are doing that day. If students will be working mostly in pairs then the desks are arranged in pairs before the students enter the room. If the activity calls for six different groups then the desks will be arranged in groups of six and so on…

Since I do quite a bit of group work, I find that doing it this way saves time and actually reduces classroom management problems.

19. What is your favorite thing about teaching?

<u>Tips:</u>

- This is a personal question, but you obviously want to say something positive and it would be a good idea to mention something about working with children. Refer back to your philosophy of teaching.

<u>Sample Answer:</u>

Before I entered the teaching profession, I worked in the restaurant business for several years. While I was successful, there was always something missing. What I love about teaching is that goes way beyond a simple paycheck. I love the idea that I have a direct impact on the future of our society.

But what I really like best is the way the kids keep me young. While many people think I am nuts for wanting to teach middle school, I find this is a great age to teach. The kids are old enough that you can discuss very serious topics as we often do in social studies, but they are still young enough to joke with them about cartoons on Nickelodeon.

20. What is your favorite part of your curriculum?

Tips:

- Many people going up in front of an interview committee are worried that they will be asked content specific questions. The fact is: That *rarely* happens. For example, if you are a social studies teacher applying for a U.S. history position it is very unlikely to hear the question, "Name two causes and two effects of the War of 1812." It is much more likely that you will be asked a more generic question such as, "What is your favorite part of the curriculum?"

- Again, this is a great opportunity to plug some of your favorite lessons and teaching strategies.

Sample Answer:

- My favorite unit to teach is World War II. I find it is very easy to make connections about what we are studying in class and what is going on in the world today. This makes it much easier to increase student motivation to learn.

- Learning about World War II also makes it easy for students to understand the importance of studying history in general…that we study history so we can learn from the mistakes and successes of our past. In fact, as part of our World War II unit I have students write a five-paragraph essay on the causes of World War II, but in this essay they must also address what the United States and/or it's allies could have done differently to prevent World War II from ever starting in the first place.

- Also, many of the students enter the unit already having an interest in the topic, either because of family members' involvement in the war or from Hollywood movies…either way, their background knowledge of the content makes it significantly easier to teach.

21. Tell me about your most rewarding teaching experience.

Tips:

- If you have been teaching for a while this should be an easy question to answer. However, if you have little or no experience, pull something from your student teaching or from another profession or volunteer activity in which you worked with children.

Sample Answer:

That's easy. My most rewarding teaching experience actually happened outside of the classroom while we were on our eighth-grade field trip to Washington D.C—which I was the team leader in organizing.

This one particular year, a young girl in my class took an immediate interest in social studies. She always stayed after class to ask me a question or tell me something about her father. Her father had been in the Vietnam War. Not only was he in the war, but he did several tours of duty and stayed on to do intelligence work afterwards. I think he was there for over ten years. Needless to say, I can't even begin to imagine the things that this man saw in his lifetime.

Unfortunately, life back in the United States after the war was not easy and, according to this student, her mom and dad did not get along too well and neither did she.

However, as the year progressed her relationship with her father started to change. She told me it was because of the stuff she was learning in my class. I guess she finally had something to talk to him about. The further along we got in the curriculum, the more they had to talk about. When we finally began our unit on the Vietnam War their relationship was at an all-time high.

At the end of the year we take our students on a two-night, three-day trip to Washington D.C. When we were about to arrive at the Vietnam War Memorial, it hit me. I called Cathy over and talked to her about the Vietnam Wall with all the names of the fallen soldiers and how people can trace over the names. I asked her if she wanted to call her dad to see if there were any names he wanted her to trace. As it turns out, this man, who had been in Vietnam for over ten years, had never been to the "wall" because it was just too difficult for him. Anyway, he gave her two names. We looked them up, found them on the wall together, and she traced both of them for her father. This was by the far the most rewarding experience for me as a teacher. Through my class and my action, I actually brought a father and daughter closer together. That is something I can carry with me for the rest of my life.

22. What extra-curricular activities do you participate in?

Tips:

- If you do not have any teaching experience yet, you will likely be asked this question in different way, such as: "What extracurricular activities *would* you be interested in?" Even though you are applying for a classroom teaching position, the reality is the job involves much more than what you do *in* the classroom. Administrators want to know that you are willing to go the extra mile. Therefore, be prepared beforehand with a couple of extra-curricular activities that you might be interested in.

- If you are you are an experienced teacher then hopefully you have participated in several extra-curricular activities. If not, you need to be able to explain why. Remember, the competition for the job may be very tough. You need to separate yourself from the pack. Extracurricular activities can make a big difference.

- Extra-curricular activities include: sports teams coaching, yearbook, newspaper, drama club, class trip coordinator, science fair, student council, choir, and teacher mentor. What is offered in each school will vary with size of the school, available staff, parental involvement, and administration's commitment to extracurricular activities.

<u>Sample Answer:</u>

I think being involved in extra-curricular activities is important Teachers build a bond with the students outside the regular classroom. It is great to work with students and see them interact in a different setting.

While at Springs School I quickly became involved in many activities outside of the classroom. The biggest job I had was eighth grade advisor. I was responsible for running the school trip and the graduation ceremony. Both of these were large tasks. The trip was a three-day, two night trip to Washington D.C. that involved quite a bit of fundraising. The trip was fairly expensive, about $550 per student. We gave the kids every opportunity to raise all of the money plus extra money for spending.

However, this meant organizing and running at least one major fundraiser each month as well as being responsible for over seventy students for three days in Washington D.C.

The other part of being the eighth grade advisor was organizing the eighth grade graduation. Since Springs School was a K to 8 school, graduation was big deal. We really put on quite a ceremony with awards, scholarships, speeches, and diplomas.

However, the extra curricular activity I enjoyed the most was being the coordinator for the eighth grade video. I worked with a team of approximately eight students who give up their lunch and recess time at least once a week to work on a video that was presented at the eighth grade graduation. We started filming from the first week of school using a digital video camera and we did all the editing on the computer. Working with the kids in this environment was really a lot of fun. Plus, the video is the highlight of graduation ceremony. I have an extra copy of last year's video that I can leave with you so you can watch it yourself. (Yes, I would actually give them a copy of the video to keep for themselves.)

23. How do you feel that your past teaching experience/student-teaching has prepared you for this job?

Tips:

- Remember, *everything* is a learning experience. If you had a horrible student teaching placement then explain how you learned what *not* to do. Sometimes bad experiences can be the best learning opportunities.

- Use this opportunity to mention people who had a positive influence on you and definitely use this opportunity to "name drop".

<u>Sample Answer:</u>

During my student teaching I had two different placements. The first one was with a high school teacher. We had very different philosophies of education. We had a good working relationship, but in reality, I was really learning what not to do as a teacher. She literally went page by page from the textbook. The students would read a section from the text for homework then answer the section review questions. The following day in class, she would lecture about what they had read the night before. I remember feeling a bit frustrated because I was taking all these great graduate classes about cooperative learning and active learning, but I wasn't seeing any of that.

My second placement, which by the way was in the same school, was absolutely fantastic. It was by far my best academic learning experience. The teacher, Joe Smith (notice the "name drop"... if he is a well respected educator the people who are interviewing you may know him too) was a master. I immediately took over two seventh grade classes. We worked on lessons every day together. He was already using many of the strategies I was learning in my graduate courses. This really helped prepare me for teaching as it gave me the opportunity to combine the theory of what I was learning in graduate school with actual classroom practice.

24. What do you think is the best asset that you could bring to this school?

<u>Tips:</u>

- Think about your own personal qualities...what makes you the person you are.

- Use this opportunity to plug anything else not yet mentioned and use one of those examples that highlight your strengths and results you have and can continue to achieve.

Sample Answer:

I have a very strong work ethic and I have been a leader at my old school for the past five years. As I said before I have taken on a leadership role with the students by being the eighth grade advisor. I have also taken on a leadership role with the staff by being involved in staff development as teacher mentor. During the school year, I was responsible for presenting one or two workshops for staff members. Throughout the year, I would work one-on-one with a new teacher. We would meet roughly once a week to discuss lesson planning, teaching strategies, and the everyday ins and outs of the school. I was responsible for conducting observations and giving feedback several times per year. In fact, this is what led me to write my first book called *Become an Effective Teacher in Minutes: Best Teaching Practices You Can Use Now*. This, in turn, developed into a side business. I now have few different books related to teaching. I've brought extra copies of these too. *(Yes, I would hand them a copy of Become an Effective Teacher in Minutes: Best Teaching Practices You Can Use Now)*.

25. Why should I hire you?

Tips:

- Well…hopefully you have already made it very clear why you should be hired ☺.

- If you are inexperienced think about this…"Passion is something that can *not* be taught". While sitting on interview committees over the past several years the issue of experience, or lack of experience, of a potential employee is one that comes up often. Many times people on the committee are overly concerned about this. My argument has always been this: *I can teach someone how to teach, what I can't teach is passion. You either have it or you don't. I'll take someone who is willing to learn and has that passion in their eyes over experience any day of the week.*

- If you are an experienced teacher then talk about that extra something that you bring with you. When I was being interviewed for my current position at Haile Middle School I acknowledged the fact that there were 140 people applying for the same position and that they had the luxury of being as picky as they wanted. Then I quickly rehashed my extra-curricular involvement with the students and professional development work with the staff.

Sample Answer:

While I may not have much practical experience in the classroom, what I do have is a passion for teaching. I think that is something that you either have or don't have. I don't think you can teach passion. I also have a deep desire to continue to learn and grow. In fact, I guarantee you I will be a better teacher in my twentieth year than I was in my second year. When you combine my passion for education and my desire to learn and grow, I think that gives me the extra something you may be looking for.

Many of the above questions are fairly generic. You should also be prepared for more specific questions with actually hypothetical situations.

Also, look out for questions from left field.

- What position would you play on a baseball team?
- What is the most creative thing you have ever done outside of teaching?
- Why should I NOT hire you?

Sometimes administrators just want to see how well you think on your feet and process the question rather than evaluating the answer content.

When answering questions, try to refer back to a portfolio as much as possible. This way, you can use specific examples (lesson plans, student work...) to answer questions. Remember, showing an actual lesson plan that exemplifies "curriculum integration" goes a long way towards answering a question on that topic. And, just imagine how much more powerful your answer becomes if you can also show examples of *student work* with that lesson plan.

Final Note on Interview Questions

In this chapter I provided what I believe are the 25 most common interview questions with tips and sample answers for each question.

Obviously, there are many more possible questions that could be asked of you.

Do a quick Google search for "teacher interview questions". You will likely find a hundred more possible questions.

It would be impossible for me to provide sample answers for every possible question that may be asked during your interview. However, if you follow the above advice and relate all your answers to specific lessons you should do great regardless of the question.

Questions that <u>You</u> Should Ask during an Interview

Just like you will be fielding questions from your interviewer, it is best to ask a few questions of your own. It shows that while you are genuinely interested in working at their school, you do have some concerns of your own. This helps give you a more confident appearance. It lets your interviewers know that not just any job will do for you, but that you want the *right* job, the *best* job. In other words, *you* are looking for the teaching position that is the best fit for *you*.

Keep your questions simple and polite. Make sure that you are asking specific questions about the position and/or work environment. Steer clear of asking any personal questions or any questions that are not directly job related. You may even want to jot down some of the answers that you are given for reference later on.

Here are some questions that you <u>should</u> ask your prospective employer:

1. Why is the position available right now?

2. What would you most like to see done in the next six months?

3. What are the most difficult problems this job entails?

4. How much freedom do I have in the curriculum decision-making process?

5. What changes do you envision in the near future for this school?

6. How many periods do I teach per day? Planning periods?

7. Do I have my own classroom?

8. What extracurricular activities can I get involved with?

9. How is your technology department? Do I have access to Internet/computer?

10. What is the school's philosophy on inclusion?

11. What is the typical class size?

12. Do you have a new teacher mentor program?

Obviously, you do not have to ask all of these questions. Instead, pick three to six that you are truly curious about. If you have done research you may know part of the answer. For example: I am aware that your school has a teacher mentor program. Could you explain how this works and how I might become involved in this program.

Questions Employers <u>Cannot</u> Ask

There are many questions that an interviewer cannot ask. Some questions are actually illegal. Many people don't realize that there are "off-limit" questions for employers.

If you do encounter some of these questions and do not feel comfortable responding you can politely ask how the question pertains to the position you're applying for. Here is a list of the questions that are illegal for an interviewer to ask:

1. Questions about your age.

2. Questions about your marital status.

3. Whether or not you have children, and/or your childcare plans.

4. Questions about your personal health.

5. Questions about your ethnicity.

6. Questions about your sexual preference.

7. Questions related to your religious beliefs and/or practices.

Basically, personal information cannot be asked by an interviewer. It is illegal, and you do not have to respond.

Closing the Interview
and the Post Interview Follow-up

Closing the Interview

Once all the questions have been asked, it is important that you end the interview well. The hard part is over and now all that is left is for you to close out the interview in the same winning manner. The first and last sentences of an interview are the ones which leave a lasting impression on the interview panel.

Wait until your interviewer stands up or requests that you do. Thank the interviewer for taking the time to see you. Offer another firm handshake, calling each interviewer by name. Ask when you should expect to hear from them about their decision.

The Post Interview Follow-up

I cannot stress enough the importance of the post interview follow-up. The follow-up can literally be the difference between getting the job and not getting the job. In fact, that is precisely what happened with my replacement at Springs School. As you may or may not know, Springs School is in the highly competitive Long Island market. It wasn't long after I told Springs about my decision to leave that we got flooded with applications. We literally had stacks of resumes to go through before we narrowed it down to a handful we would call for interviews.

The plan was to interview a handful of candidates and then bring two or three back to give sample lessons.

Well, as you can imagine, we had a number of excellent candidates for the position. After the first round of interviews, we narrowed it down to four. Our plan was to call back only three for sample lessons. One of the three had strong connections and was at least going to be given a shot (sorry, but that's reality!) Two of the other candidates were both local and both male.

Being local on the East End of Long Island is extremely important as the traffic and the commute from further "up-island" can kill you. The fact, that both were men also gave them a little something extra because the middle school at the time was almost all women. Don't get me wrong! We were still looking for the best candidate and the best one would get the job. Everything else being equal, the school was hoping to replace me with another male teacher.

The fourth, and final, candidate was a woman who was not local. In fact, she would have to make quite a long commute every day. The fear was that she would not be able to put in the hours that the position demanded. It would just be a matter of time before she found a job closer to home. (By the way, you can forget about a new teacher moving to the east end of Long Island to be closer to the school. A fixer-upper shack costs at least $600,000!)

So, it looked as if our decision was made. We would ask the candidate with the connections and the two other male candidates back to give sample lessons. Let me stress: *All three of these candidates were excellent. Each would have made a nice addition to the school.*

However, this is not what our *fourth* candidate had in mind. She made every effort *after* the interview was over to make sure she got an opportunity to give a sample lesson.

First, she sent a hand-written thank you note to each member of the committee the very next day. Two days later she sent a follow-up email. She even called and spoke to one of the committee members a couple of days after that.

She was so thorough *and* enthusiastic that we decided to give her a chance with her sample lesson.

Guess who got the job?

That's right! Candidate number four blew everyone else out of the water. Her sample lesson was head and shoulders above the rest. There was no possible way that we were not going to offer her the position. The funny thing is, if not for her post-interview follow-up, someone else would have that job right now.

So, once the interview is finished, don't make the mistake of thinking that you're done. Start by sending a thank you note to each member of the committee thanking them for their time and consideration.

Now, while I would actually rather receive an *email* "thank you", there are many who disagree and believe that email is too impersonal and takes no thought or effort. However, I think those days are quickly coming to an end. Nevertheless, it is better to be safe and send an actual handwritten thank you note. *(This is the "post-interview cover letter" that was discussed earlier. If you have information that might be interesting to them, an article or reference material/site include that with the letter to help differentiate yourself)*

If you haven't heard from the employer within a week, you should call the office to ask if the interview panel has reached a decision yet. This is not being pushy. It demonstrates your enthusiasm and persistence. If they haven't reached a decision, ask when you might expect to hear from them. If they don't give an answer, try again in another week.

The Telephone Interview

It is not particularly common for schools to conduct interviews over the phone. Phone interviews are usually saved for jobs that include sales and/or jobs that are not so easily applied for by the other methods. However, the telephone interview is becoming a bit more common as more teachers are beginning to relocate from state to state, province to province and country to country. A traditional, face-to-face interview may be difficult to put together. It is possible, therefore, that a school will offer an interview by phone.

In fact, that is exactly how I got my current job at Haile Middle School. I was relocating from New York to Florida. Instead of having me fly down for the interview I was interviewed over the phone by the principal and vice-principal.

There are both advantages and disadvantages to the phone interview. You should be aware of both:

<u>Advantages</u>

- Have everything laid out in front of you. Use a large table to spread everything out before the phone interview starts. For example, you should have several sample lesson plans out and easily accessible, any questions you may want to ask, water, this ebook ☺ etc. While these are things you would have at a traditional in-person interview, when it is over the phone you can spread these things out and access them much more easily.

- Dress for comfort. No need to worry about what you look like if the interview is over the phone. Take advantage of that by wearing clothes you are truly comfortable in.

- You can move around the room. For me this is a big advantage! I am a "pacer". Whenever I am on the phone, I like to pace back and forth. (It helps me think.)

Disadvantages

- Distractions. Make sure to lock the door, get the kids, spouse, and barking dogs out of the house! Turn off your call waiting. Nothing should come between you and that phone call.

- Not being able to "read" your interviewer. This is by far the biggest disadvantage of the phone interview. In a face-to-face interview, it is fairly easy to tell if your potential employer likes how you are answering questions by his or her facial expressions. Obviously, if you sense that the interviewer likes where you are headed with an answer then you can keep going into more depth. On the other hand, if you sense displeasure you can stop what you are saying or find a way to re-phrase your intended meaning.

Unfortunately, with the phone interview, it is nearly impossible to "read" the interviewer. What's worse, if you are on speakerphone, those interviewing you can communicate with each other by making facial expressions and passing notes to each other without you knowing. For this reason, I see the phone interview as a huge disadvantage over the traditional face-to-face interview. Avoid it whenever possible.

** **Note:** The phone interview I had with Haile Middle School was the most difficult interview I have ever been part of, regardless of which side of the table I was sitting on.

Last-minute Tips

Hopefully, by now, you are much more confident and have learned what you need to know to ace your next interview. However, here are some last-minute tips and hints that may help you out...

    ** **Note:** Many of these tips came from a recent teacher interview discussion panel that was held as part of the Alternative Certification Program at Manatee Community College where I teach as an adjunct professor. The panel is made up of myself and four administrators (1 elementary, 2 middle school, and 1 high school).

- Definitely hand-deliver your resume. An administrator MAY very well interview you on the spot. Two of the administrators on the panel admitted that, for certain teaching positions, they have their secretaries contact them immediately if someone comes in to drop off a resume.

- If you are substitute teaching to get your foot in the door remember: Every day is a job interview. Dress the part. Become part of the school community, and make contacts!

- Make as many contacts as you can. This is a teacher's greatest resource when trying to land a teacher interview. A phone call from a teacher or another administrator—even if they don't know the each other—will often get you the interview.

- Research the school and the district!! Administrators want to know that you have done your homework. You should know everything you possibly can about that school/district. Know the mission statement and any major current initiatives that are underway in the school district.

- Research the people conducting the interview. Just as much as they want a quality teacher, they want someone that they can work well with...they are looking for a relationship...a good fit!

- They will Google you! Therefore, make sure to Google yourself and see what comes up.

- Get rid of your Facebook account!!

- Have a professional email address. Don't make silly mistakes like having an email such as sexylove69@aol.

- Even the high school administrators want to know how teachers get parents involved. Yes, the high school administrator expects teachers to call parents too!

- Be prepared to explain how you cover something that you are NOT interested in. Many teachers prepare for the question, "Take me through one of your *favorite* lessons.". But, the administrators on the discussion panel always ask, "How would you teach something that you do *not* enjoy teaching but must." This is a great question, because the reality is: You will not enjoy teaching every part of your curriculum.

- Market your skills and related experience to the position that you are applying for. Be sure to do it in a way that is positive and not arrogant.

- Bring your list of questions with you in a folder with the school's name on it so that you don't forget them. You should also keep your extra resumes in there too.

- Since some interviewers may ask you what your biggest fault might be. You should pick a fault that is actually a good thing. Try saying "I don't take on projects that I can't give 110% on." Or, "I'm a bit of a workaholic. Failing to save time for myself is my biggest fault." Or, "I am a perfectionist. In order to have the best learning experience, I frequently spend inordinate amounts of time on a lesson plan." Or, "Sometimes I am so excited about the skills my students are learning that I go home and rattle on about my job. I must consciously make time for my home life."

- Let your interviewer bring up the topic of salary first. If you have done your homework, you know what to expect.

- Don't volunteer your personal opinions to your interviewer... *Especially politics!*

- Try to establish a good rapport with your interviewer. Be casual but professional, and, most importantly, BE YOURSELF!

- Treat the interview like a meeting — with a purpose to find mutual fit.

- Remember to interview the "employer" too!

- Try to answer questions in behavioral-based responses.

- Here are three steps to guide you:
  - Explain the task/situation/problem
  - Describe what you did; and

- What was the outcome?

- Remember to ask for the job! Demonstrate your confidence and interest to be on the team.

- Once you land your position remember to thank your network and keep it active — change is continuous these days.

Summary

By now, you have learned:

- How to find out about teaching positions.
- How to get the interview.
- How to prepare for the interview.
- How to make a great first impression.
- How to build the best resume.
- How to create a winning cover letter.
- What to do during a telephone interview.
- What question you will be asked during an interview.
- What questions *you* should ask during an interview.
- What questions *cannot* be asked during an interview
- How to follow up on your interview

Remember: while this guide gives you the inside secrets and has greatly increased your chances of landing that perfect teaching position, nothing looks quite as impressive to a potential employer as someone who is well versed in using a variety of teaching strategies and methods.

For an arsenal of effective teaching strategies that will not only help you get the job, but more importantly, will enable you to have that fulfilling teaching career you've always dreamed of, make sure to read my other books:

**Become an Effective Teacher in Minutes:
Best Teaching Practices You Can Use Now**

How to Succeed as an Elementary Teacher

"*Marjan, you are making a difference in the lives of students and in the world.*" Harry Wong

HOW TO
SUCCEED
AS AN
ELEMENTARY
TEACHER

With a foreword by Jack Canfield

MARJAN GLAVAC

www.TheBusyEducator.com

Teaching Is... Moments that inspire and Motivate Teachers to Make a Difference

Now go out there and get that job!

Teacher and Job Search Resources

Here are the teacher resources that accompany this book. To download your bonus resources, visit:

http://thebusyeducator.com/guide.htm

Job Search Resources

FREE Access to How To Get A Teaching Job Course

If you want to learn the strategies I used to land my dream teaching job, get them now!

By the end of the course you'll:

- Acquire the skills to get the teaching job you want

- Learn valuable research techniques for the teaching market

- Confidently ace your teacher interview

- Understand what principals are looking for in teacher candidates

- Create a unique teacher interview

- Get your resume and cover letter read by the right people

100+ Practice Questions for Teacher Interviews

Acquire the skills to get the teaching job you want and learn valuable research techniques for the teaching market.

This powerful guide reveals the most common teaching job interview questions. It's divided into the following sections for easy access to the information you need:

- Getting to Know You Questions
- Questions about Your Education and Student Teaching
- Personal Information
- Interview Questions about Teaching Style
- Interview Questions about Parent/Teacher Communication
- Teacher Interview Questions related to Differentiating Instruction
- Questions related to Classroom Management and Final Interview Questions

Top 10 Secrets of the World's Greatest Cover Letter... Attract Job Interviews Like a Magnet

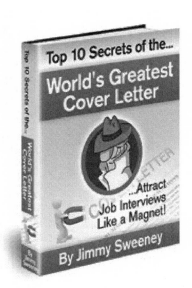

If you want to discover some of the greatest "think-outside-the-box" job search strategies ever revealed, get your copy right now.

- The Greatest Cover Letter Secret of All

- How to DOUBLE Your Job Search Odds

- Big Word WARNING!

- The Powerful 'Post Interview' Letter

- ASKING For The Job Interview

Top 10 Secrets YOU Can Use To Ace Any Job Interview...
Unique job interview tips to get you hired fast!

Discover…

- Top Ten Traits of Superior Employees
- Why Volunteering Adds Value
- Precise and Concise… That's Nice!
- How To Bridge Those Trouble Spots
- Sell Your Skills—and Yourself

Top 10 Secrets YOU Can Use To Ace Any Job Interview...
Unique job interview tips to get you hired fast!

Find out...

- The Best-Kept Interview Secret
- How to Block Stress—BEFORE the Interview
- What NOT To Do During an Interview
- Be Prepared! Secret Tools to Bring to an Interview
- Preparing for a Job Interview—Mentally

Networking

The Better (and More Fun!) Way to Find a Job Networking. This power point presentation is a complete guide to networking.

Inside you'll find:

- Specific questions to ask for a successful informational interview

- How to effectively network at networking events

- The best way to make an email introduction

- Quick ways to promote yourself

Teacher Resources

- Proactive Classroom Management e-Course

  ~ Get access to my special report: How To Take Control In Your Classroom And Put An End To Constant Fights And Arguments. Learn the *proactive* approach to classroom management with this **FREE** 5-part e-course. Apply the strategies taught in this course and you will see an immediate and definite decrease in classroom management problems.

Teaching Tips Machine Newsletter

~ *FREE* weekly teaching tips to improve your career.

The Busy Educator Facebook Fan Page

~ Stop by the Fan Page and discuss *ANYTHING* related to teaching. Hope to see you there.

One more thing…

Enjoyed This Book?

You Can Make A Difference

Thank you very much for purchasing this book *The Complete Guide to Getting A Teaching Job*. I'm very grateful that you chose this book from all the other wonderful books on the market.

I hope this book made your life as an elementary teacher that much more enjoyable for you and your students. If it did, please consider sharing your thoughts with your fellow teachers on Facebook, Twitter, LinkedIn and Instagram.

If you enjoyed this book and found value in reading it, please take few minutes to post an honest review for the book. Reviews are very important to readers and authors — and difficult to get. Reviews don't have to be long: even a sentence or two is a huge help. Every review helps.

While on your favorite review site, feel free to vote for helpful reviews. The top-voted reviews are featured for display, and most likely to influence new readers. You can vote for as many reviews as you like.

All the best,

Adam Waxler and Marjan Glavac

Appendix A: Sample Cover Letter

April 17, 2019
Mr. John Wortham
610 S Del Prado Blvd.
Cape Coral, Fl 33990

Dear Mr. John Wortham:

I have been working for the past five years as the eighth-grade social studies teacher at Springs Junior High School in East Hampton, New York.

Unfortunately, New York does not provide the quality of life that my family desires. After spending several vacations, over several years, touring the state of Florida, my family has decided to relocate. At the close of this school year we will be moving to Fort Myers. I have recently received my letter of eligibility for a Florida teaching certification and have applied for the Caloosa Middle School Social Science position using the Lee County online application process.

As a future member of the Fort Myers community, I would appreciate an opportunity to discuss my philosophy of education and the possibility of filling the vacant social science position.

I have enclosed my resume and philosophy statement and encourage you to call my references. I have also included a CD-ROM with a complimentary copy of my ebook, *eTeach: A Teacher Resource for Learning the Strategies of Master Teachers*. Reading this ebook will give you a real insight to my knowledge and use of the most effective teaching strategies, as well as my dedication to the teaching profession.

Thank you for your time.

Sincerely,

Adam Waxler

Appendix B: Sample Resume

Adam S. Waxler
2 Cedar Street
East Hampton, NY 11937
(631) 834-1396
waxler@optonline.net

EDUCATION M.S. Ed. Elementary Education (3.95 GPA) *Long Island*

University

Certification Secondary Social Studies (4.0 GPA) *Long Island*

University, 2000

B.A. Political Science, *St. Lawrence University*, 1992

PROFESSIONAL Teacher: *Springs Public School*, East Hampton, NY,

EXPERIENCE September 2000–Present

Teach 7th & 8th Grade Social Studies

- Designed and successfully implemented several interdisciplinary social studies-language arts units
- Designed and successfully implemented an A/B block schedule
- Created 7th & 8th grade social studies curriculum maps
- Designed and conducted a full day 9/11 workshop
- Successful use of *History Alive* curriculum materials to promote cooperative interaction, increase learning, and improve social skills
- Innovative implementation of state standards
- Thorough knowledge of the New York State Grade 8 Intermediate-Level Social Studies Test
- Thorough knowledge of DBQ

8th Grade Advisor

- Coordinate 8th Grade Class Trip
- Coordinate 8th Grade Graduation Ceremony
- Coordinate 8th Grade Beach Picnic

8th Grade Video Advisor

- Supervise and guide students in creating and editing a year-long 8th grade digital video project

Teacher Mentor

- Train new teaching staff
- Present workshops on effective teaching strategies

Buddy Program

Adam S. Waxler

RELATED Books

Become an Effective Teacher in Minutes: Best Teaching Practices You Can Use Now

<u>Newsletter Publisher:</u> *The Teaching Tips Machine*

<u>Computer Capability:</u> Web design, internet marketing, digital video editing

REFERENCES

Mr. Tom Quinn, *Superintendent*, Springs School District,

East Hampton, NY (631) 324-4243

Mrs. Nancy Carney, *Assistant Superintendent*, Riverhead School District, Riverhead, NY (631) 329-0945

Mr. Chris Sarlo, *Principal,* Springs School District,

East Hampton, NY (631) 324-5282

Mrs. Lisa Seff, *Science Teacher*, Springs School District,

East Hampton, NY (631) 324-2392

Ms. Maria Mondini, *Math Teacher*, Southampton School District,

Southampton, NY (631) 329-6694

Mrs. Amy Turner, *Social Studies Teacher*, Springs School District

East Hampton, NY (631) 537-2471

Ms. Emily Ragusa, *English Teacher*, Springs School District,

East Hampton, NY (631) 276-9017

Mr. Adam Osterweil, *English Teacher*, Springs School District,

East Hampton, NY (631) 907- 2898

Mrs. Margaret Garsetti, *ESL Teacher*, Springs School District, East Hampton, NY (631) 324-0789

Mr. Eric Weiss, *Math Teacher,* retired, Springs School District, East Hampton, NY (802) 899-290

Appendix C: Sample Philosophy Statement

Adam Waxler
2 Cedar Street
East Hampton, NY 11937
(631) 834-1396

Philosophy Statement

Children do not learn through authoritarian teaching or through the passive memorization of fragmented bits of information. The mastery of a subject involves much more than "hammering" learning in, it involves learning through experience and solving complex problems that model learning outside of school. Let's face it, in the real world what we *experience* are *complex problems*.

Students learn best when they actively construct meaning around their interests and experiences. In this way students gain a deeper understanding of material. The use of worksheets, textbooks, and lectures designed only to fill students with information leads to passive learning and rote memorization and places too much emphasis on short-term recall ability. As an educator, I want to free my students from relying on the teacher for answers so they can begin to learn on their own and continue to learn after school is over. My goal is to create lifelong learners who understand and appreciate that learning does not stop once the test is taken.

In order to reach *all* students, a teacher must use a variety of teaching techniques to meet the various learning styles of the students and must therefore be both flexible and approachable. Teachers should work more as an aid, or a guide, that facilitate the learning process, rather than as omnipotent instructors who attempt to force knowledge into the minds of their students. Information should not just be passed down as if it is the last and all-knowing word. Instead, the classroom must be student-centered with a high degree of interaction between the students and between the teacher and student.

I strongly believe that *all* students can learn when teaching takes this interest-based, differentiated approach. However, making connections to student interests does not mean the entire curriculum must revolve around the interests of the student, but rather, these connections must be made within a core academic curriculum. By applying this conservative curriculum through a liberal teaching methodology, we are combining *what* children should learn with *how* they should learn it, thus creating lifelong learners out of all our children.